THE COMPLETE BOOK OF

ITALIAN COOKING

THE COMPLETE BOOK OF
ITALIAN COOKING

Edited by
Veronica Sperling & Christine McFadden

SMITHMARK

Distributed in the USA by SMITHMARK Publishers,
a division of U.S. Media Holdings Inc.,
16, East 32nd Street, New York, NY 10016

SMITHMARK books are available for bulk purchase for sales promotion and premium
use. For details, write or call the manager of special sales, SMITHMARK publishers,
16 East 32nd Street, New York, NY 10016; (212) 532-6600

ISBN: 0-76519-686-7

10 9 8 7 6 5 4 3 2 1

Printed in Italy

Produced by Haldane Mason, London

Acknowledgements
Art Direction: Ron Samuels
Design: Digital Artworks Partnership Ltd

Material contained in this book has previously appeared in
Italian Farmhouse Cooking by Judy Bugg
Italian Regional Cooking and *Soups & Broths* by Rosemary Wadey
Pasta Dishes by Pamela Westland
Pizzas by Wendy Lee
Sensational Salads by Carole Handslip
Vegetarian Main Meals by Kathryn Hawkins
Additional recipes by Kathryn Hawkins

Contents

ITALIAN CUISINE

Tourists flock in their millions to Italy, drawn by the ancient Roman architecture, the wealth of art galleries and churches, the famous Renaissance paintings, and carefully restored frescos by Michelangelo on the ceiling and walls of the Sistine Chapel in the Vatican, Rome. They also go to enjoy the warm, friendly atmosphere and the food!

A CULINARY HISTORY

The Italian cuisine that we know today is the result of a very checkered history. Over the centuries, many different races from all over Europe invaded or traveled through the Italian peninsula bringing with them new culinary ideas. The Etruscans brought polenta and the Greeks introduced wonderful seafood cookery. The Romans not only developed the Greek style of cookery, but wrote down their recipes – and they still exist today.

In 1861, the Unification of Italy brought twenty separate provinces under one flag, but the different regional styles of cooking remained largely unchanged.

ITALIAN FOOD REGION BY REGION

The most significant divide for Italy's cuisine is that between the industrial north and the poorer south. The north, with its fertile plains, its mountains, and lakes, produces good quality wines and dairy foods. By contrast, the sunnier, rockier south is home to olive groves, eggplant, tomatoes, and herbs. Although there are regional differences in the cuisine, they do have features in common: the ingredients are fresh, techniques are simple, recipes are traditional, and cooking, even in restaurants, is home-style.

Piedmont

The name means "at the foot of the mountain", which it is, bordering on both France and Switzerland. Its fertile arable fields are irrigated by the many canals which flow through the region.

The food is substantial, peasant-type fare, though the wildly expensive fragrant white truffle is found in this region. Truffles are finely flaked or grated and added to many of the more sophisticated dishes. There is an abundance of wild mushrooms and a wide variety of game. Garlic features strongly in the recipes, and polenta, gnocchi, and rice are eaten in larger quantities than pasta, the former being offered as a first course when soup is not served.

Lombardy

The mention of Milan, the capital of the province, produces immediate thoughts of the wonderful risotto named after the city and also the Milanese soufflé flavored strongly with lemon. Veal dishes, including *vitello tonnato* and *osso buco*, are specialities of the region, and other excellent meat dishes, particularly pot roasts, feature widely. The lakes of the area produce a wealth of fresh fish. Rice and polenta are popular, but pasta also appears in many guises. The famous sweet yeasted cake *panettone* is a delicious product of this region.

Trentino-Alto Adige

This is an area of mountains, rich green valleys, and lakes where fish are plentiful. There is a strong German influence, particularly when it comes to the wines. There are also several German-style liqueurs produced, such as Aquavit, Kümmel, and Slivovitz. The foods are robust and basic. Pasta, as well as simple meat and variety meat dishes, is popular, particularly in the Trentino area. In the Adige, soups and pot roasts are favored, often with added dumplings and spiced sausages.

Veneto

The cooking in this north-east corner is straightforward, with generous portions of polenta served with almost everything. The land is intensively farmed, providing mostly cereals and wine. Pasta is less in evidence, with polenta, gnocchi,

and rice more favored. Fish is in abundance and especially good seafood salads are widely available. There are also excellent robust soups and risottos flavored with the seafood and sausages of the area.

Liguria

The Genoese are excellent cooks, and all along the Italian Riviera can be found excellent trattorias which produce amazing fish dishes flavored with the local olive oil. Pesto sauce flavored with basil, cheese, and pine nuts comes from this area, along with other excellent sauces. Fresh herbs are widely used in many dishes, including the famous pizzas – their aroma is unmistakable.

Emilia-Romagna

This is a special region of gastronomic excellence characterized by an abundance of rich food. Tortellini and lasagne are among the many pasta dishes which feature widely, as do *saltimbocca* and other veal dishes. Parma is famous for its ham, *prosciutto di Parma*, thought to be the best in the world. Modena is famous for balsamic vinegar, which has grown in popularity over the past decade. The vinegar is distilled from wine until it becomes dark brown and develops an extremely rich flavor.

Tuscany

The Tuscans share the Emilians great pride in cooking and eating, and are known to have hefty appetites. Tuscany has everything: an excellent coastal area providing splendid fish, hills covered in vineyards, and fertile plains where every conceivable vegetable and fruit happily grow.
There is plenty of game in the region, providing many interesting recipes.
Tripe cooked in a thick tomato sauce is popular, as well as many liver dishes. Beans appear frequently in many guises, and there are richly flavored pot roasts, steaks, and full-bodied soups. Florence boasts a wide variety of specialties, such as the hefty char-cooked T-bone steak *bistecca alla Fiorentina*, while Siena is the home of the famous candied spiced fruit cake *panforte di Siena*.

Umbria/Marches

Although not especially spectacular, the cuisine of inland Umbria is noted for its pork and the use of local fresh ingredients of excellent quality. These include lamb, game, and freshwater fish from the lakes. Spit-roasting and broiling are popular, and the excellent local olive oil is used both in cooking and to pour over dishes before serving. Black truffles, olives, fruit, and herbs are plentiful and feature in many recipes. Eastward to the Marches, the food tends to be more elaborate with almost every restaurant noted for its excellent cuisine. The wealth of fish from the coast adds to the variety, as do first-class sausages and cured pork. Pasta features widely all over the region.

Lazio

Rome is the capital of both Lazio and Italy, and thus has become a focal point for specialties from all over the country. The cooking is characterized by robust flavors and rich sauces, but dishes tend to be fairly simple and quick to prepare, hence the many pasta dishes with delicious sauces, and gnocchi in various forms. There are also plenty of dishes featuring lamb, veal (*saltimbocca* being just one), and variety meats, all with generous amounts of herbs and seasonings. Vegetables and fantastic fruits are always in abundance in the local markets; and beans appear in soups and many other dishes.

Abruzzi and Molise

Formerly counted as just one region called Abruzzi e Molise, these regions have a mountainous interior with river valleys, high plateaux, densely forested areas, and a coastal plain. The cuisine here is deeply traditional, with local hams and cheeses from the mountain areas, interesting sausages with plenty of garlic and other seasonings, cured meats, and wonderful fish and seafood. Lamb features widely: tender, juicy, and well-flavored with herbs.

Campania

Naples is the home of pasta dishes, served with a splendid tomato sauce (with many variations) famous worldwide. Pizza is said to have been created in Naples and now has spread to the north of the country, and indeed all over the world.
Fish abounds, with *fritto misto* and *fritto pesce* being great favorites, varying daily depending on the catch. Fish stews are robust and varied, and shellfish in particular is often served with pasta. Cutlets and steaks are excellent, served with strong sauces usually flavored with garlic, tomatoes, and

herbs: pizzaiola steak is one of the favorites. Excellent mozzarella cheese is produced locally and used to create the crispy *mozzarella in carozza*, again served with a garlicky tomato sauce. Sweet dishes are popular too, often with flaky pastry and ricotta cheese, and the seasonal fruit salads laced with wine or liqueur take a lot of beating.

Puglia (Apulia)

The ground is stony but it produces good fruit, olives, vegetables, and herbs, and, of course, there is a large amount of seafood. Puglians are said to be champion pasta eaters: many of the excellent pasta dishes are exclusive to the region, both in shape and ingredients. Mushrooms abound and are always added to the local pizzas.

Oysters and mussels are plentiful, and so is octopus. Brindisi is famous for its shellfish – both the seafood salads and risottos are truly memorable. But it is not all fish or pasta: lamb is roasted or stewed to perfection and so is veal, always with plenty of herbs.

Basilicata

This is a sheep-farming area, mainly mountainous, where potent wines are produced to accompany a robust cuisine largely based on pasta, lamb, pork, game, and abundant dairy produce. The salamis and cured meats are excellent, as are the mountain hams. Lamb is flavored with the herbs and grasses on which it feeds. Wonderful thick soups – true minestrone – are produced in the mountains, and eels and fish are plentiful in the lakes.

Chili peppers are grown in this region and appear in many of the recipes. They are not overpoweringly strong, although the flavors of the region in general tend to be quite strong and intense. The cheeses are excellent, good fruit is grown, and interesting local bread is baked in huge loaves.

Calabria

This is the toe of Italy, where orange and lemon groves flourish, along with olive trees and a profusion of vegetables, especially eggplant, which are cooked in a variety of ways.

Chicken, rabbit, and guinea fowl are often on the menu, as are pizzas, often with a fishy topping. Mushrooms grow well in the Calabrian climate and feature in many dishes from sauces and stews to salads. Pasta comes with a great variety of sauces, including baby artichokes, eggs, meat, cheese, mixed vegetables, the large sweet bell peppers of the region, and of course garlic. The fish is excellent too, with fresh tuna and swordfish available, as well as many other varieties.

Like most southern Italians, the Calabrians are sweet-toothed. Many desserts and cakes are flavored with aniseed, honey, almonds, and the plentiful figs of the region.

Sicily

This is the largest island in the Mediterranean and the cuisine is based mainly on fish and vegetables. Fish soups, stews, and salads appear in unlimited forms, including tuna, swordfish, mussels, and many more. Citrus fruits are widely grown, as well as almonds and pistachio nuts. The local wines, including the dark, sweet dessert wine Marsala, are excellent.

Meat is often given a long, slow cooking, or else is ground and shaped before cooking. Game is plentiful and is often cooked in sweet-sour sauces containing the local black olives. Pasta abounds again, with more unusual sauces as well as the old favorites.

All Sicilians have a love of desserts, cakes, and especially ice-cream. Cassata and other ice-creams from Sicily are famous all over the world, and the huge variety of flavors of both ice creams and granita makes it difficult to decide which is your favorite.

Sardinia

A pretty island with a wealth of flowers in the spring, but the landscape dries out in the summer from the hot sun. The national dish is suckling pig or newborn lamb cooked on an open fire or spit. Rabbit, game, and variety meat dishes are also very popular. Fish is top quality, with excellent sea bass, lobsters, tuna, mullet, eels, and mussels in good supply.

The sweet dishes are numerous and often extremely delicate, and for non-sweet eaters there is fresh fruit of almost every kind in abundance.

The island has a haunting aroma which drifts from many kitchens. It is myrtle (*mirto*), a local herb which is added to anything and everything, from chicken to the local liqueur. Along with the wonderful cakes and breads of Sardinia, myrtle will long remain a memory of the island when you have returned home.

GETTING TO KNOW PASTA

Many of the popular pasta dishes have their origins in Italy where pasta has been produced since the thirteenth century or earlier. The word pasta simply means "paste" or "dough" in Italian. The principal ingredients of traditional pasta are modest, although today there are more and more types of fresh and dried pasta available. By far the most popular type is made from durum wheat, which is milled to form fine semolina grains, and then extruded through drums fitted with specially perforated disks, producing 600 different pasta varieties.

VARIETIES OF PASTA

Pasta is made from either the endosperm of wheat, or from the whole wheat grain, which contains more dietary fiber. The addition of spinach paste produces an attractive green color – *lasagne verde* is a popular example; tomato paste produces a deep coral coloring.

As well as green and red pasta, there are other colors available: saffron pasta is an attractive yellow-orange color, beet-hued pasta is a deep pink, and pasta colored with squid ink is a dramatic black which makes any dish truly eye-catching. You can also buy or make pasta flecked with chopped basil or other herbs. *Pasta all'uovo*, made with eggs, is a rich yellow and produced in a range of shapes, both fresh and dried. Pasta is also made from ground buckwheat which gives the product a grayish color and nutty flavor that combines well with vegetable and herb sauces.

Apart from these refinements of color and flavor, pasta is generally divided into four main categories: long and round pasta, ribbons, tubes and shapes. Since dried pasta has a shelf life of up to six months (page 12) and fresh pasta may be frozen for up to six months, it is a good idea to build up your own selection of varieties with which to surprise your family and friends.

The following is a glossary of some of the different types of pasta:

ANELLI, ANELLINI small rings used for soup

BOZZOLI deeply-ridged, cocoon-like shapes

BUCATINI long, medium-thick tubes

CAPPELLETTI wide-brimmed hat shapes

CAPPELLI D'ANGELO "angel's hair", thinner than cappellini

CAPPELLINI fine strands of ribbon pasta

CASARECCIA short, curled lengths of pasta twisted at one end

CAVATAPPI short, thick corkscrew shapes

CONCHIGLIE ridged shells

CONCHIGLIETTE little shells used for soup

CORNETTI ridged shells

CRESTI DI GALLO curved shapes

DITALI, DITALINI short tubes

ELICHE loose spiral shapes

ELICOIDALI short, ridged tubes

FARFALLE bows

FEDELI, FEDELINI fine tubes twisted into "skeins"

FESTONATI short lengths, like garlands

FETTUCCINE ribbon pasta, narrower than tagliatelle

FIOCHETTE, FIOCHELLI small bow shapes

FREZINE broad, flat ribbons

FUSILLI spindles, or short spirals

FUSILLI BUCATI thin spirals, like springs

GEMELLI "twins", two pieces wrapped together

GRAMIGNA meaning "grass" or "weed"; the shapes look like sprouting seeds

LASAGNE flat, rectangular sheets

LINGUINI long, flat ribbons

LUMACHE smooth, snail-like shells, good with seafood sauces

LUMACHINE U-shaped flat noodles

MACARONI, MACCHERONI long or short-cut tubes, may be ridged or elbow-shaped

MALTAGLIATI triangular-shaped pieces, traditionally used in bean soups

ORECCHIETTE dished ear shapes

ORZI tiny, rice-like grains used in soups

PAPPARDELLE widest ribbons, either straight or sawtooth-edge

PEARLINI tiny rounds

PENNE short, thick tubes with diagonal-cut ends

PIPE RIGATE ridged, curved pipe shapes

RIGATONI thick, ridged tubes

RUOTI wheels

SEMINI seed shapes

SPAGHETTI fine, medium or thick rods

SPIRALE two rods twisted into spirals

STROZZAPRETI "priest strangler", double twisted strands

TAGLIARINI flat ribbon, thinner than tagliatelle

TAGLIATELLE broad, flat ribbons

TORTIGLIONE thin, twisted tubes

VERMICELLI fine, slender strands usually sold folded into "skeins"

ZITI TAGLIATI short, thick tubes

NUTRITIONAL VALUE OF PASTA

Pasta has frequently had to answer to the charge that it is a fattening food which must be be avoided by anyone who is on a weight-reducing diet. The answer to that charge is that it may not be the pasta that piles on the calories, but more likely some of the sauces we choose to serve with it.

This table shows you some approximate dietary and nutritional credentials of dry uncooked pasta.

	per 3½ oz
Protein	⅖ oz
Fat	1/25 oz
Dietary fiber	⅛ oz
Carbohydrate	2⅖ oz
Calories	342

Basic Pasta Dough

Making your own pasta dough is time consuming but immensely satisfying. You will need plenty of space for the rolled-out dough, and somewhere to hang it to dry. Serves four.

1 cup strong all-purpose flour, plus extra for dusting
⅔ cup fine semolina
1 tsp salt
2 tbsp olive oil
2 eggs
2–3 tbsp hot water

Sieve the flour, semolina, and salt into a bowl and make a well in the center. Pour in half the oil and add the eggs. Add 1 tablespoon of hot water and, using your fingertips, work to a smooth dough. Sprinkle on a little more water if necessary to make the dough pliable.

Lightly dust a board with flour, turn the dough out, and knead it until it is elastic and silky. This could take 10–15 minutes. Dust the dough with more flour if your fingers become sticky.

Alternatively, put the eggs, 1 tablespoon hot water, and the oil in the bowl of a food processor and process for a few seconds. Add the flour, semolina, and salt and process until smooth. Sprinkle on a little more hot water if necessary to make the dough pliable. Transfer to an electric mixer and knead using the dough hook for 2–3 minutes.

Divide the dough into two equal pieces. Cover a counter with a clean cloth or dishcloth and dust it liberally with flour. Place one portion of the dough on the floured cloth and roll it out as thinly and evenly as possible, stretching the dough gently until the pattern of the weave shows through. Cover it with a cloth and roll out the second piece in a similar way.

Use a ruler and a sharp knife blade to cut long, thin strips for noodles, or small confectionery cutters to cut rounds, stars, or other decorative shapes.

Cover the dough shapes with a clean cloth and leave them in a cool place (not the refrigerator) for 30–45 minutes to become partly dry. To dry ribbons, place a dishcloth over the back of a chair and hang the ribbons over it.

Pasta machines

If you get caught up in the enthusiasm of pasta-making, you might like to buy a machine to roll, stretch, and cut the dough. The method is to feed the pasta repeatedly through the rollers, one notch thinner each time. This is time-consuming but important, as the pasta needs to keep its elasticity.

To roll the pasta from the Basic Pasta Dough recipe (page 11), first divide the dough into two pieces. Roll until all the pieces have gone through the machine at each setting. If the strips become too long and unwieldy, cut them into manageable lengths.

Lay the pasta out on dishcloths to dry until it feels leathery, which is when it is ready to be cut. The machine will cut pasta into strips for ribbon pasta; other shapes will have to be cut by hand. Place a dishcloth over the back of a chair and hang the strips to dry, then use immediately.

Cooking pasta

The real enjoyment of pasta depends upon the cooking time. Undercooked, it will be unyielding and taste of raw flour; overcooked, it will be soft and sticky. The Italians describe the perfect texture as *al dente*, meaning that the pasta is tender but still slightly resistant to the bite.

Cooking times vary according to the type and volume of the pasta, and you should always follow the times recommended on the packet. In general, fresh pasta will be cooked in 3–5 minutes; dried pasta in 6–7 minutes for fine strands, such as vermicelli; 7–12 minutes for quick-cooking macaroni, spaghetti, and noodles; and 10–15 minutes for cannelloni tubes and sheets of lasagne.

Whatever the pasta type, have ready a large pan of water at a steady, rolling boil. Add salt and 1 tablespoon of olive oil to prevent sticking. Add the pasta gradually, a handful or a few strands at a time so that the water continues to boil and the pasta is kept separate. Do not completely cover the pan, or the water will boil over. Leave it uncovered, or partly covered. Drain the cooked pasta into a colander and, if it is not to be served at once, return it to the pan with a little olive oil.

How much to allow

It is difficult to calculate exactly how much pasta to allow for each serving. For a first course or salad, 1–2 oz dried pasta per person is about right, and 3–4 oz dried pasta for a main dish. It is worth remembering that dried pasta more than doubles in

volume during cooking, absorbing water until it is rehydrated. Fresh pasta will not absorb so much.

Storing and freezing pasta

Dried pasta will keep in good condition for up to six months. Keep it in the packet, and reseal it once you have opened it, or transfer the pasta to an airtight jar.

Fresh pasta has a very short storage life, only one or two days in the refrigerator, so buy it only when you want to serve it. Otherwise it can be frozen for up to six months.

Cooked pasta may be stored for up to three days in the refrigerator. If the pieces have stuck together, turn them in a colander and run warm water through them. Drain well, then toss the pasta in hot olive oil or melted butter before serving. Cooked pasta may be frozen for up to three months but must be thawed at room temperature before reheating.

PASTA SAUCES

Creative cooks will enjoy partnering their favorite sauces with a variety of pastas. Although there are classic combinations, such as Spaghetti Bolognese and Spaghetti Carbonara, there are no rules, just guidelines which are largely a matter of practicality, appearance, and taste. For example, long ribbons or round pasta give tomato- or oil-based sauces something to cling to, while shapes and hollow tubes are ideal for trapping chunkier sauces in their crevices. Béchamel and cheese sauces add creamy richness and moisture to baked pasta dishes.

Basic Tomato Sauce

2 tbsp olive oil
1 small onion, chopped
1 garlic clove, chopped
14 oz can chopped tomatoes
2 tbsp chopped parsley
1 tsp dried oregano
2 bay leaves
2 tbsp tomato paste
1 tsp sugar
salt and pepper

Heat the oil in a pan over a medium heat and fry the onion until translucent. Add the garlic and fry for another minute.

Stir in the chopped tomatoes, parsley, oregano, bay leaves, tomato paste, sugar, and salt and pepper.

Bring the sauce to a boil, then simmer, uncovered, for 15–20 minutes until the sauce has reduced by half. Taste the sauce and adjust the seasoning if necessary. Discard the bay leaves just before serving.

Béchamel Sauce

1¼ cups milk
2 bay leaves
3 cloves
1 small onion
¼ cup butter, plus extra for greasing
6 tbsp flour
1¼ cups light cream
large pinch of freshly grated nutmeg
salt and pepper

Pour the milk into a small pan and add the bay leaves. Press the cloves into the onion, add to the pan, and bring the milk to a boil. Remove from the heat and set it aside to cool.

Strain the milk into a pitcher and rinse the pan. Melt the butter in the pan and stir in the flour. Stir for 1 minute, then gradually pour on the milk, stirring constantly. Cook the sauce for 3 minutes, then pour on the cream, and bring it to a boil. Remove from the heat and season to taste with nutmeg, salt, and pepper.

Lamb Sauce

2 tbsp olive oil
1 large onion, sliced
2 celery stalks, thinly sliced
1 lb lean lamb, ground
3 tbsp tomato paste
5 oz bottled sun-dried tomatoes, drained and chopped
1 tsp dried oregano
1 tbsp red wine vinegar
⅔ cup chicken stock
salt and pepper

Heat the oil in a skillet over a medium heat and fry the onion and celery until the onion is translucent. Add the lamb and fry, stirring frequently, until it browns.

Stir in the tomato paste, sun-dried tomatoes, oregano, vinegar, and stock. Season with salt and pepper.

Bring to a boil and cook, uncovered, for 20 minutes or until the meat has fully absorbed the stock. Taste and then adjust the seasoning if necessary.

Cheese Sauce

2 tbsp butter
1 tbsp flour
1 cup milk
2 tbsp light cream
pinch of freshly grated nutmeg
salt and pepper
1½ oz sharp hard cheese, grated
1 tbsp freshly grated Parmesan

Melt the butter in a pan, stir in the flour, and cook for 1 minute. Gradually pour on the milk, stirring all the time. Stir in the cream and season the sauce with nutmeg, salt, and pepper.

Simmer the sauce for 5 minutes to reduce, then remove it from the heat, and stir in the cheeses. Stir until the cheeses have melted and blended into the sauce.

Italian cheeses for pasta

Some cheeses have a natural affinity with pasta dishes and appear frequently in recipes.

RICOTTA A milky white, soft, and crumbly Italian cheese similar to cottage cheese. It is low in fat, being made from whey, but some varieties produced now have whole milk added. If you cannot obtain Ricotta, use another low-fat soft cheese. To obtain a smooth-textured sauce or filling press through a strainer.

PARMESAN A mature and exceptionally hard cheese, Parmesan is the most important of flavorings for pasta. It may be useful to have a small carton of ready-grated Parmesan in the refrigerator, but you will find that it quickly loses its pungency and "bite". For that reason, it is better to buy small quantities of the cheese in one piece and grate it yourself. Tightly wrapped in plastic wrap and foil, it can be kept in the refrigerator for several months. Grate it just before serving, for maximum flavor.

PECORINO A hard ewe's milk cheese which resembles Parmesan and is often used for grating over dishes. It has a sharp flavor and is only used in small quantities.

MOZZARELLA Another highly popular cheese, this is a soft cheese, with a bland flavor, traditionally made from water buffalo's milk. Buffalo's milk is now scarce, and so this cheese is often made with cow's milk. It can be used fresh, most popularly in salads, and also provides a tangy layer in baked dishes or a topping for pizzas.

Olive oil

Olive oil, which is at the heart of so many Italian dishes, has a personality all of its own, and each variety has its own characteristic flavor.

EXTRA-VIRGIN OLIVE OIL This is the finest grade, made from the first, cold pressing of hand-gathered olives. Always use extra-virgin oil for salad dressings.

VIRGIN OLIVE OIL This oil has a fine aroma and color, and is also made by cold pressing. It may have a slightly higher acidity level than extra-virgin oil.

REFINED OLIVE OIL This is made by treating the paste residue from the pressings with heat or solvents to extract the residual oil.

OLIVE OIL OR PURE OLIVE OIL This is a blend of refined and virgin olive oil.

GETTING TO KNOW PIZZAS

The pizza has become a universally popular food, in every form from the genuine article – thin, crisp, and oven-baked – to frozen and fast-food pizza slices. The delightful aroma of freshly baked pizza topped with tomatoes, fresh herbs, and cheese rarely fails to have a mouthwatering effect.

History of the Pizza

Although there is much speculation about where pizza in its simplest form was first invented, it is usually associated with the old Italian city of Naples. It was then a simple street food, richly flavored and quickly made. It was not always round and flat as we know it today, but was originally folded up like a book, with the filling inside, and eaten by hand. Pizzas were usually sold on the streets by street criers who carried them around in copper cylindrical drums kept hot by coals from the pizza ovens.

The word "pizza" actually means any kind of pie. The classic Napoletana pizza is probably the best-known of the many varieties. This consists of a thin crust of dough topped simply with a fresh tomato sauce, Mozzarella cheese, olives, anchovies, and a sprinkling of oregano. When baked, the flavors blend perfectly together to give the distinctive aromatic pizza. Another classic is the "Margherita" pizza, named after the Italian Queen Margherita. Bored with the usual cuisine when on a visit to Naples, she asked to sample a local speciality. The local "Pizzaiolo" created a pizza in the colors of the Italian flag – red tomatoes, green basil, and white Mozzarella. The Queen was delighted, and it became widely celebrated.

As well as its being economical and popular, few other dishes are as versatile as the pizza, thanks to the countless possible permutations of bases and toppings that can be served to suit every palate and every occasion.

Fortunately for the busy cook, pizzas are an easy food to chill or freeze, ready to be cooked on demand. There is a wide range of ready-made pizza bases as well as dry mixes which only need the addition of water before they are ready for kneading and baking.

Pizzas are also sold complete with a variety of toppings, which you can bake as they are, or add more toppings yourself. Although they never seem to taste so good as a real homemade pizza, these can be very useful to keep on hand. Jars of bell peppers, sun-dried tomatoes, and artichokes in olive oil make very good toppings, and will keep for quite a while in your larder.

The dough base

Although making your own base can be a little time-consuming, the method is very straightforward, and you end up with a delicious home-baked dish, as well as a sense of achievement. The ingredients are very basic:

YEAST There are three types of yeast available: fresh, dried, and easy-blend. Fresh is usually found in health-food stores and is not expensive. Buy it in bulk and freeze in ½ oz quantities ready to use whenever needed.

Dissolve ½ oz fresh yeast in 6 tbsp tepid water with ½ tsp sugar, and allow it to froth before adding it to the flour – about 5 minutes. The frothiness indicates that the yeast is working. Fresh

yeast will keep for 4–5 days in the refrigerator. Make sure it is well covered, as it will dry out very quickly.

Dried yeast is sold in packets or tubs by most supermarkets. It has a shelf-life of about six months, so buy only a small tub if you are not going to make bread dough on a regular basis. Like fresh yeast, add it to the tepid water with a little sugar, and stir to dissolve. Allow the mixture to stand for 10–15 minutes until froth develops on the surface.

Easy-blend yeast is the simplest to use as it is simply stirred dry into the flour before the water is added. It is sold in packets by most supermarkets.

FLOUR Traditional pizza bases are made from bread dough, which is usually made with strong plain bread flour. You could also use one of the many types of whole wheat flours available, such as stoneground whole wheat, wheatmeal, and granary. Try adding a handful of wheatgerm or bran to white flour for extra flavor, fiber, and interest. Or you could mix equal quantities of whole wheat and white flour.

Always sift the flour first, as this will remove any lumps and help to incorporate air in the flour, which will, in turn, help to produce a light dough. If you sift whole wheat flours, there will be some bran and other bits left in the strainer, which are normally tipped back so that their goodness and fiber are added to the sifted flour.

Yeast thrives in warm surroundings, so all the ingredients and equipment for the dough should be warm. If tepid yeast liquid is added to a cold bowl containing cold flour, it will quickly cool down. This will retard the growth of the yeast, and the dough will take much longer to rise. If the flour is kept in a cool cupboard or larder, remember to get it out in enough time for it to warm to room temperature before you use it. Sift the flour into a large mixing bowl, then place it somewhere warm, such as an in the oven on the lowest setting. However, do not allow it to overheat, as this will kill the yeast.

SALT Add the required amount of salt to the flour when sifting, as this will help to distribute it evenly throughout the resulting mixture. Salt is important, as it helps to develop the gluten in the flour. Gluten is the protein which produces the characteristic elasticity of the dough, but mostly it provides the dough with its flavor.

WATER It has been said that Naples produces the best pizzas because of the quality of its water! But as that may be rather far to travel just to make a pizza, your local water will have to suffice. The water must be tepid, as this is the optimum temperature for the yeast to grow. Take care to add just the right amount of water stated in the recipe. If you add too much water, the dough will be difficult to handle and the cooked base will be too hard.

OIL For the best flavor always use a good-quality olive oil, such as extra virgin.

Kneading the dough

This can be the most daunting procedure but it is a very necessary one. The kneading process mixes all the ingredients together and strengthens the gluten, which holds the bubbles of air created by the yeast, which cause the dough to rise. The best way of doing it is to take the edge of the dough that is furthest away from you and pull it into the center toward you, then push it down with the heel of your hand, turning the dough round with your other hand as you go. The dough must be kneaded for at least 10 minutes, or until it becomes very smooth and pliable and is no longer sticky. If time is short, knead the dough in a food processor for a few minutes.

Place the dough in an oiled bowl, turning once so the surface is coated. Cover with plastic wrap and leave to rise in a warm place for 1–2 hours until doubled in size.

Bread dough bases can be kept for several days before being used. After kneading, carefully wrap in plastic wrap to prevent them from drying out in the refrigerator. Allow extra time for the dough to rise, as it will take a while for the dough to warm up and for the yeast to begin to work.

Toppings

There are a number of classic ingredients that are used regularly in pizza toppings. These include tomato sauce, olives, anchovies, capers, mushrooms, bell peppers, artichokes, and chilies, as well as cheese and herbs. Be adventurous and experiment, but don't be afraid to stick to simple combinations of just two or three ingredients. The simplest pizzas are often the most delicious and memorable as the flavors don't fight each other.

When making pizza for several people with differing tastes, place different toppings on separate sections of the pizza, or make individual ones in a selection of flavors. They can all cook at the same time, making it easy to suit all tastes.

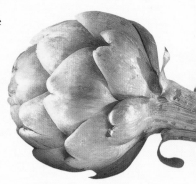

TOMATO SAUCE Most pizzas have tomato sauce as the basis for the topping. This can be made using either canned or fresh tomatoes. There are many types of canned tomatoes available –

for example, whole plum tomatoes, chopped tomatoes, or chopped strained tomato (passata). Canned chopped tomatoes may have added ingredients, such as garlic, basil, onion, chili, and mixed herbs, which will add more interest to the sauce. Make sure the sauce is well seasoned before spreading it on the base, as a tasteless sauce will spoil your pizza.

The sauce will keep well in a screw-top jar in the refrigerator for up to a week, or can be frozen if you need to keep it for longer periods.

CHEESE The cheese most often associated with the pizza is, of course, Mozzarella. It is a mild, white, delicate cheese traditionally made from buffalo milk. The best feature of this cheese as far as pizzas are concerned is its ability to melt and produce strings of cheese when a slice is cut and pulled away. It is sold in supermarkets, wrapped in small bags of whey to keep it moist. Slice, grate, or cut it into small pieces before placing it on the pizza. Many supermarkets stock bags of pre-grated Mozzarella cheese, which is a great timesaver.

The other cheeses most often found on pizzas are hard cheeses, such as Parmesan. If you are using strongly flavored topping ingredients, such as anchovies and olives, a milder-tasting cheese may be more suitable. Experiment with different cheeses to suit your taste.

HERBS Whenever possible, use fresh herbs. They are readily available, especially since the introduction of "growing" herbs – small pots of herbs which you can buy from the supermarket and grow at home. This not only ensures the herbs are as fresh as possible, but also provides a continuous supply.

If you use dried herbs, remember that you need only about one third of dried to fresh. The most popular pizza herbs are basil, oregano, and parsley, although you can experiment with your favorite ones. Torn leaves of fresh basil on a tomato base is a simple but deliciously aromatic combination.

Successful baking

The secret of a crisp, chewy base is to bake pizzas at a very high temperature for as short a time as possible. Traditionally, pizzas are cooked in special ovens on a stone hearth. A large peel or paddle is used to slide them in and out. Baking on a pizza stone produces the best results at home. Alternatively, use a cookie sheet or a perforated pizza pan – the holes allow heat and air to reach the center of the base, resulting in a crisp, evenly-cooked crust.

Grease the pizza pan or cookie sheet well, to prevent the pizza from sticking. Always push up the edge of the dough to form a rim to prevent the topping from spilling over while it cooks.

Serving

Pizzas should be served as soon as they leave the oven as the cheese will set slightly and lose its elasticity as it cools down. Use a couple of large slices to transfer the pizza to the serving plate. Use a warm serving plate to prevent the pizza from going cold too quickly.

Cut the pizza into wedges or strips using a sharp knife or pizza cutter. As pizza slices are easy to eat by hand, they make great party food.

Crisp salads, coleslaw, and garlic bread are ideal accompaniments and help to make a balanced meal. Because of their rich flavor pizzas are best served with Italian table wine, such as Valpolicella, Chianti, or a well-chilled Frascati. If you are not a wine drinker, beer will go with pizza just as well.

Follow a pizza meal with a refreshing dessert, such as fresh fruit salad, sorbet, or ice cream. Zabaglione, a light Italian dessert of eggs, sugar, and Marsala wine, makes a perfect ending.

Freezing

Pizzas are ideal standby food, as you can make and freeze them in advance, and both the bread dough and the complete pizza can be frozen. Make up double quantities of dough and freeze the half that is unused after it has been kneaded. Wrap in plastic wrap and place in a freezer bag. Defrost at room temperature and allow to rise as normal. Alternatively, rise and roll out the dough, top with tomato sauce, cheese, and any other topping ingredients, and bake for only 10 minutes. Cool, wrap in a plastic bag, and place in the freezer. Cook straight from the freezer in a hot oven for about 15 minutes.

ANTIPASTI & ACCOMPANIMENTS

The word antipasto means "before the main course" and what is served may be simple and inexpensive or highly elaborate. Antipasti usually come in three categories: meat, fish, and vegetables. There are many varieties of cold meats, including ham, invariably sliced paper-thin. All varieties of fish are combined for the antipasto di pesce, including inkfish, octopus, and cuttlefish. Huge shrimp, mussels, and fresh sardines are always popular.

Numerous vegetables feature in Italian cuisine and are an important part of the daily diet. They are served as an antipasto, as an accompaniment to the meat or fish course, or occasionally as a course of their own. They are prepared in a variety of ways – raw or marinated, deep-fried or pickled, with and without dressings. Always cook vegetables only until "al dente" and still slightly crisp. That way, they retain more nutrients and the colors remain bright, contrasting appealingly and deliciously with other parts of the meal.

Mediterranean Bell Pepper Salad

Colorful marinated Mediterranean vegetables make a tasty starter.
Serve with fresh bread or Tomato Toasts.

SERVES 4

INGREDIENTS

1 onion
2 red bell peppers
2 yellow bell peppers
3 tbsp olive oil
2 large zucchini, sliced
2 garlic cloves, sliced
1 tbsp balsamic vinegar
1¾ oz anchovy fillets, chopped
¼ cup black olives, halved and pitted
1 tbsp chopped fresh basil
salt and pepper

TOMATO TOASTS

small stick of French bread
1 garlic clove, crushed
1 tomato, peeled and chopped
2 tbsp olive oil
salt and pepper

1 Cut the onion into wedges. Core and deseed the bell peppers, and cut into thick slices.

2 Heat the oil in a large heavy-based skillet. Add the onion, bell peppers, zucchini, and garlic, and fry gently for 20 minutes, stirring occasionally.

3 Add the vinegar, anchovies, olives, and seasoning to taste, mix thoroughly, and leave to cool.

4 Spoon onto individual plates and sprinkle with the basil.

5 To make the tomato toasts, cut the French bread diagonally into ½ in. slices.

6 Mix the garlic, tomato oil, and seasoning together, and spread thinly over each slice of bread.

7 Place on a cookie sheet, drizzle with the olive oil, and bake in a preheated oven, 425°F, for 5–10 minutes until crisp.

Step *1*

Step *2*

Step *3*

Preserved Meats (Salumi)

*Mix an attractive selection of these preserved meats (Salumi) with olives
and marinated vegetables for extra color and variety.*

SERVES 4

INGREDIENTS

3 ripe tomatoes
3 ripe figs
1 small melon
2 oz Italian salami, sliced thinly
4 thin slices mortadella
6 slices prosciutto
6 slices bresaola
4 fresh basil leaves, chopped
olive oil
½ cup marinated olives, pitted
freshly ground black pepper, to serve

1 Slice the tomatoes thinly.

2 Cut the figs into fourths.

3 Halve the melon, scoop out the seeds, and cut the flesh into wedges.

4 Arrange the meats on one half of a serving platter. Arrange the tomato slices in the center and sprinkle with the basil leaves and oil.

5 Cover the rest of the platter with the fruit and scatter the olives over the meats.

6 Serve with a little extra olive oil to drizzle over the bresaola, and coarsely ground black pepper.

Step *1*

Step *2*

Step *4*

Mozzarella in Carozza

A delicious way of serving Mozzarella – the cheese stretches out into melted strings as you cut into the Carozza.

SERVES 4

INGREDIENTS

7 oz Mozzarella
4 slices prosciutto, about 3 oz
8 two-day old slices white bread,
crusts removed
butter for spreading
2–3 eggs
3 tbsp milk
vegetable oil for deep-frying
salt and pepper

TOMATO AND PEPPER SAUCE

1 onion, chopped
2 garlic cloves, crushed
3 tbsp olive oil
1 red bell pepper, cored, deseeded, and chopped
14 oz can peeled tomatoes
2 tbsp tomato paste
3 tbsp water
1 tbsp lemon juice
salt and pepper
flat-leaf parsley, to garnish (optional)

1 First make the sauce: fry the onion and garlic in the oil until soft. Add the bell pepper and continue to cook for a few minutes. Add the tomatoes, tomato paste, water, lemon juice, and seasoning. Bring to a boil, cover, and simmer for 10–15 minutes or until tender. Cool the sauce a little, then purée or liquidize until smooth, and return to a clean pan.

2 Cut the Mozzarella into 4 slices as large as possible; if the cheese is a square piece cut into 8 slices. Trim the prosciutto slices to the same size as the cheese.

3 Lightly butter the bread and use the cheese and ham to make 4 sandwiches, pressing the edges firmly together. If liked, they may be cut in half at this stage. Cover with plastic wrap and chill.

4 Lightly beat the eggs with the milk and seasoning in a shallow dish.

5 Carefully dip the sandwiches in the egg mixture until well coated, and leave to soak for a few minutes if possible.

6 Heat the oil in a large pan or deep-fryer until it just begins to smoke, or until a cube of bread browns in about 30 seconds. Fry the sandwiches in batches until golden brown on both sides. Drain well on crumpled paper towels and keep warm. Serve the sandwiches hot, with the reheated tomato and pepper sauce, and garnished with parsley.

Step *3*

Step *5*

Step *6*

Black Olive Pâté

This pâté is delicious served as a starter on crisp tomato bread. It can also be served as a cocktail snack on small rounds of fried bread.

SERVES 4

INGREDIENTS

1½ cups pitted juicy black olives
1 garlic clove, crushed
finely grated rind of 1 lemon
4 tbsp lemon juice
½ cup fresh bread crumbs
¼ cup full-fat soft cheese
salt and pepper
lemon wedges, to garnish

1 Roughly chop the olives and mix with all the other ingredients, except the salt and pepper. Pound until smooth, or place in a food processor and work until fully blended. Season to taste with salt and freshly ground black pepper.

2 Store in a screw-top jar and chill for several hours before using – this allows the flavors to develop.

3 For a delicious cocktail snack, use a cookie cutter to cut out small rounds from a thickly sliced loaf.

4 Fry the bread rounds in a mixture of olive oil and butter until they are a light golden brown. Drain on paper towels.

5 Top each round with a little of the pâté, garnish with lemon wedges, and serve immediately. This pâté will keep chilled in an airtight jar for up to 2 weeks.

Step *1*

Step *3*

Step *4*

Roast Bell Pepper Salad

Serve chilled as an antipasto with cold meats, or warm as a side dish.
Garlic bread makes a delicious accompaniment.

SERVES 4

INGREDIENTS

4 large mixed red, green, and yellow bell peppers
4 tbsp olive oil
1 large red onion, sliced
2 garlic cloves, crushed
4 tomatoes, peeled and chopped
pinch of sugar
1 tsp lemon juice
salt and pepper

1 Trim and halve the bell peppers and remove the seeds.

2 Place the bell peppers skin-side up under a preheated hot broiler. Cook until the skins char. Rinse under cold water and remove the skins.

3 Trim off any thick membranes and slice thinly.

4 Heat the oil and fry the onion and garlic until softened. Then add the bell peppers and tomatoes and fry over a low heat for 10 minutes.

5 Remove from the heat, add the sugar and lemon juice, and season with salt and pepper to taste. Serve immediately or leave to cool. The flavors will continue to develop as the salad cools.

Step 2

Step 3

Step 4

Seafood Salad

Seafood is plentiful in Italy and varieties of seafood salads are found everywhere. Each region has its own specialty.

SERVES 4

INGREDIENTS

6 oz squid rings, defrosted if frozen
2½ cups water
⅔ cup dry white wine
8 oz hake or monkfish, cut into cubes
16–20 fresh mussels, scrubbed and beards removed
20 clams in shells, scrubbed, if available (otherwise use extra mussels)
4–6 oz peeled shrimp
3–4 scallions trimmed and sliced (optional)
radicchio and curly endive leaves, to serve
lemon wedges, to garnish

DRESSING

6 tbsp olive oil
1 tbsp wine vinegar
2 tbsp chopped fresh parsley
1–2 garlic cloves, crushed
salt and pepper

GARLIC MAYONNAISE

5 tbsp thick mayonnaise
2–3 tbsp fromage frais or natural yogurt
2 garlic cloves, crushed
1 tbsp capers
2 tbsp chopped fresh parsley or mixed herbs

1 Poach the squid in the water and wine for 20 minutes or until nearly tender. Add the fish and continue to cook gently for 7–8 minutes or until tender. Strain, reserving the fish. Pour the stock into a clean pan.

2 Bring the fish stock to a boil and add the mussels and clams. Cover the pan and simmer gently for about 5 minutes or until the shells open. Discard any that stay closed.

3 Drain the shellfish and remove from their shells. Put into a bowl with the cooked fish and add the shrimp and scallions if using.

4 For the dressing, beat together the oil, vinegar, parsley, garlic, salt, and plenty of black pepper. Pour over the fish, mixing well. Cover and chill in the refrigerator for several hours.

5 Arrange small leaves of radicchio and curly endive on four plates and spoon the fish salad into the center. Garnish with lemon wedges. Combine all the ingredients for the garlic mayonnaise and serve with the salad.

Step *1*

Step *2*

Step *3*

Artichoke & Prosciutto Salad

A pretty salad with a piquant flavor. Use bottled artichokes rather than canned ones if possible, as they have a better flavor.

SERVES 4

INGREDIENTS

9 fl oz bottle artichokes in oil, drained
4 small tomatoes
¼ cup sun-dried tomatoes, cut into strips
¼ cup black olives, halved and pitted
¼ cup prosciutto, cut into strips
1 tbsp chopped fresh basil

FRENCH DRESSING

3 tbsp olive oil
1 tbsp wine vinegar
1 small garlic clove, crushed
½ tsp Dijon or Meaux mustard
1 tsp clear honey
salt and pepper

1 Drain the artichokes thoroughly, then cut them into fourths, and place in a bowl.

2 Cut each tomato into 6 wedges and place in the bowl with the sun-dried tomatoes, olives, and prosciutto.

3 To make the dressing, put all the ingredients into a screw-top jar and shake vigorously until the ingredients are thoroughly blended.

4 Pour the dressing over the salad and toss well together.

5 Transfer to individual plates and sprinkle with the basil.

Step *1*

Step *2*

Step *4*

Crostini alla Fiorentina

Serve as a starter, or simply spread on small pieces of crusty fried bread (crostini) as an appetizer with drinks.

SERVES 4

INGREDIENTS

3 tbsp olive oil
1 onion, chopped
1 celery stalk, chopped
1 carrot, chopped
1–2 garlic cloves, crushed
4 oz chicken livers
4 oz calf's, lamb's, or pig's liver
⅔ cup red wine
1 tbsp tomato paste
2 tbsp chopped fresh parsley
3–4 canned anchovy fillets, chopped finely
2 tbsp stock or water
2–3 tbsp butter
1 tbsp capers
salt and pepper
small pieces of fried crusty bread, to serve
chopped parsley, to garnish

1 Heat the oil in a pan, add the onion, celery, carrot, and garlic, and cook gently for 4–5 minutes or until the onion is soft, but not colored.

2 Meanwhile, rinse and dry the chicken livers. Dry the calf's or other liver, and slice into strips. Add the liver to the pan, and fry gently for a few minutes until the strips are well sealed on all sides.

3 Add half the wine and cook until mostly evaporated. Then add the rest of the wine, tomato paste, half the parsley, the anchovy fillets, stock or water, a little salt, and plenty of black pepper.

4 Cover the pan and simmer for 15–20 minutes or until the meat is tender and most of the liquid has been absorbed.

5 Cool the mixture a little, then either coarsely grind or put it into a food processor and process to a chunky purée.

6 Return to the pan and add the butter, capers, and remaining parsley. Heat through gently until the butter melts. Adjust the seasoning and turn into a bowl. Serve warm or cold spread on the slices of crusty bread and sprinkled with chopped parsley.

Step *2*

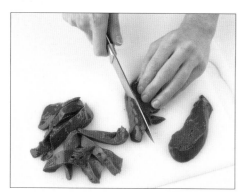

Step *3*

Step *6*

Tuna, Bean, & Anchovy Salad

*Serve as part of a selection of antipasti, or for a summer lunch
with hot garlic bread.*

SERVES 4

INGREDIENTS

1 lb tomatoes
7 oz can tuna fish, drained
2 tbsp chopped fresh parsley
½ cucumber
1 small red onion, sliced
8 oz cooked green beans
1 small red bell pepper, cored and deseeded
1 small crisp lettuce
6 tbsp French dressing
3 hard-cooked eggs
2 oz can anchovies, drained
12 black olives, pitted

1 Cut the tomatoes into wedges, flake the tuna fish, and put both into the bowl with the parsley.

2 Cut the cucumber in half lengthwise, then cut into slices. Slice the onion. Add the cucumber and onion to the bowl.

3 Cut the green beans in half, chop the red bell pepper and add both to the bowl with the lettuce leaves.

4 Pour over the French dressing and toss thoroughly, then spoon into a salad bowl to serve.

5 Cut the eggs into fourths, arrange over the top with the anchovies, and scatter with the olives.

Step *1*

Step *2*

Step *3*

Warm Pasta with Basil Vinaigrette

*Sun-dried tomatoes and olives enhance this delicious pesto-inspired
salad, which is just as tasty served cold.*

SERVES 4–6

INGREDIENTS

8 oz pasta spirals
4 tomatoes, peeled
½ cup black olives
¼ cup sun-dried tomatoes
2 tbsp pine nuts, toasted
2 tbsp Parmesan shavings
fresh basil sprig, to garnish

BASIL VINAIGRETTE

4 tbsp chopped fresh basil
1 garlic clove, crushed
2 tbsp freshly grated Parmesan
4 tbsp olive oil
2 tbsp lemon juice
pepper

1 Cook the pasta in boiling salted water for 10–12 minutes until al dente. Drain and rinse well in hot water, then drain again thoroughly.

2 To make the vinaigrette, beat the basil, garlic, Parmesan, olive oil, lemon juice, and pepper until well blended.

3 Put the pasta into a bowl, pour over the basil vinaigrette, and toss thoroughly.

4 Cut the tomatoes into wedges. Halve and pit the olives and slice the sun-dried tomatoes.

5 Add the tomatoes, olives, and sun-dried tomatoes to the pasta and mix thoroughly. Transfer to a salad bowl and scatter the nuts and Parmesan shavings over the top. Serve warm, garnished with a sprig of basil.

Step *3*

Step *4*

Step *5*

Eggplant Salad

A starter with a difference from Sicily. It has a real bite, both from the sweet-sour sauce, and from the texture of the celery.

SERVES 4

INGREDIENTS

2 large eggplants, about 2 lb
6 tbsp olive oil
1 small onion, chopped finely
2 garlic cloves, crushed
6–8 celery stalks, cut into ½ in. slices
2 tbsp capers
12–16 green olives, pitted and sliced
2 tbsp pine nuts
1 oz dark chocolate, grated
4 tbsp wine vinegar
1 tbsp brown sugar
salt and pepper
2 hard-cooked eggs, sliced, to serve
celery leaves or curly endive, to garnish

1 Cut the eggplant into 1 in. cubes and sprinkle liberally with 2–3 tablespoons of salt. Leave to stand for an hour to extract the bitter juices, then rinse off the salt under cold water, drain, and dry on paper towels.

2 Heat most of the oil in a skillet and fry the eggplant cubes until golden brown all over. Drain on paper towels, then put in a large bowl.

3 Add the onion and garlic to the skillet with the remaining oil and fry very gently until just soft. Add the celery to the skillet and fry for a few minutes, stirring frequently, until lightly colored but still crisp.

4 Add the celery to the eggplant with the capers, olives, and pine nuts and mix lightly.

5 Add the chocolate, vinegar, and sugar to the residue in the skillet. Heat gently until melted, then bring to a boil. Season with a little salt and plenty of freshly ground black pepper. Pour over the salad and mix lightly. Cover, leave until cold, and then chill thoroughly.

6 Serve with sliced hard-cooked eggs and garnish with celery leaves or curly endive.

Step *2*

Step *4*

Step *5*

Baked Fennel Gratinati

Fennel is often used in Italian cooking. In this dish its distinctive flavor is offset by the smooth besciamella.

SERVES 4

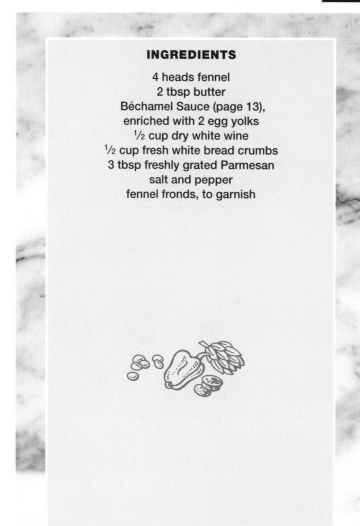

INGREDIENTS

4 heads fennel
2 tbsp butter
Béchamel Sauce (page 13),
enriched with 2 egg yolks
½ cup dry white wine
½ cup fresh white bread crumbs
3 tbsp freshly grated Parmesan
salt and pepper
fennel fronds, to garnish

1 Remove any bruised or tough outer stalks of fennel and cut each head in half.

2 Put into a saucepan of boiling salted water and simmer for 20 minutes until tender, then drain.

3 Butter an ovenproof dish liberally and arrange the drained fennel in it.

4 Mix the wine into the white sauce and season to taste. Pour over the fennel.

5 Sprinkle evenly with the bread crumbs and then the Parmesan.

6 Place in a preheated oven, 400°F, and bake for 20 minutes until the top is golden. Serve garnished with fennel fronds.

Step *1*

Step *4*

Step *5*

Baked Eggplant Parma-Style

Simmer the tomato sauce gently to reduce it slightly before using.

SERVES 4

INGREDIENTS

4 eggplants, trimmed
3 tbsp olive oil
2 × 5 oz packets Mozzarella, thinly sliced
4 slices prosciutto, shredded
1 tbsp chopped fresh marjoram
1 tbsp chopped fresh basil
½ quantity Béchamel Sauce (page 13)
¼ cup Parmesan, grated
salt and pepper

TOMATO SAUCE

4 tbsp olive oil
1 large onion, sliced
4 garlic cloves, crushed
14 oz can chopped tomatoes
1lb fresh tomatoes, peeled and chopped
4 tbsp chopped fresh parsley
2½ cups hot vegetable stock
1 tbsp sugar
2 tbsp lemon juice
⅔ cup dry white wine
salt and pepper

1 To make the sauce, heat the oil in a large saucepan. Fry the onion and garlic until just beginning to soften. Add the canned and fresh tomatoes, parsley, stock, sugar, and lemon juice. Cover and simmer for 15 minutes. Stir in the wine and season to taste.

2 Slice the eggplant thinly lengthwise. Bring a large saucepan of water to a boil and cook the eggplant slices for 5 minutes.

3 Drain the eggplant slices on paper towels and pat dry.

4 Pour half the fresh tomato sauce into a greased ovenproof dish. Cover with half the cooked eggplants and drizzle with a little oil. Cover with half the Mozzarella, prosciutto, and herbs. Season to taste.

5 Repeat the layers and cover with the white sauce. Sprinkle with the Parmesan. Bake in a preheated oven, 375°F, for 35–40 minutes until golden on top.

Step *2*

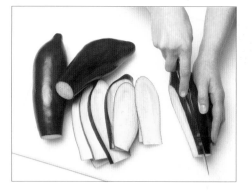

Step *3*

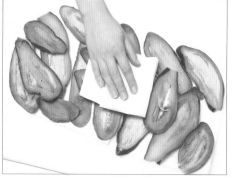

Step *4*

SOUPS

Soups are a very important part of the Italian cuisine. They vary in consistency from light and delicate to hearty main meal soups which need to be eaten with a knife and fork. Texture is always apparent – Italians rarely serve smooth soups. Some may be partially puréed, but the identity of the ingredients is never entirely obliterated. There are regional characteristics too. In the north, soups are often based on rice, while in Tuscany, thick bean or bread-based soups are popular. Tomato, garlic, and pasta soups are typical of the south. Minestrone is known world-wide, but the best-known version probably comes from Milan. However, all varieties are full of vegetables and are delicious and satisfying.

Fish soups abound in one guise or another, and most of these are village specialties, so the variety is unlimited. Many of these soups constitute a whole meal, particularly those containing a large proportion of beans, or with lightly toasted slices of bread added to the bowl. For Italians, the time of year is important in determining which soup will be served – vegetables, roots, pulses, and herbs are always chosen when they are in season and at the peak of perfection.

Minestrone with Pesto

One of the many versions of minestrone, which always contains a variety of vegetables, pasta, and rice and often includes beans.

SERVES 6

INGREDIENTS

scant 1 cup dried cannellini
beans, soaked overnight
10 cups water or stock
1 large onion, chopped
1 leek, trimmed and sliced thinly
2 celery stalks, sliced very thinly
2 carrots, chopped
3 tbsp olive oil
2 tomatoes, peeled and chopped roughly
1 zucchini, trimmed and sliced thinly
2 potatoes, diced
3 oz elbow macaroni (or other small macaroni)
salt and pepper
4–6 tbsp freshly grated Parmesan

PESTO

2 tbsp pine nuts
5 tbsp olive oil
2 bunches basil, stems removed
4–6 garlic cloves, crushed
½ cup grated Pecorino or Parmesan
salt and pepper

1 Drain the beans, rinse, and put in a saucepan with the water or stock. Bring to a boil, cover, and simmer gently for 1 hour.

2 Add the onion, leek, celery, carrots, and oil. Cover and simmer for 4–5 minutes.

3 Add the tomatoes, zucchini, potatoes, macaroni, and seasoning. Cover again and continue to simmer for about 30 minutes or until very tender.

4 Meanwhile, make the pesto. Fry the pine nuts in 1 tablespoon of the oil until pale brown, then drain. Put the basil into a food processor or blender with the nuts and garlic. Process until well chopped. Alternatively, chop finely by hand and pound with a pestle and mortar. Gradually add the oil until smooth. Turn into a bowl, add the cheese and seasoning, and mix thoroughly.

5 Stir 1½ tablespoons of the pesto into the soup until well blended. Simmer for a further 5 minutes and adjust the seasoning. Serve very hot, sprinkled with the cheese.

Step *2*

Step *3*

Step *5*

Red Bean Soup

Beans feature widely in Italian soups, making them hearty and tasty. You can use other varieties of beans in this soup, if preferred.

SERVES 4–6

INGREDIENTS

scant 1 cup dried red kidney beans,
soaked overnight
7½ cups water
1 large ham bone
2 carrots, chopped
1 large onion, chopped
2 celery stalks, sliced thinly
1 leek, trimmed, washed, and sliced
1–2 bay leaves
2 tbsp olive oil
2–3 tomatoes, peeled and chopped
1 garlic clove, crushed
1 tbsp tomato paste
4 tbsp Italian rice
4–6 oz green cabbage, shredded finely
salt and pepper

1 Drain the beans and put into a saucepan with enough water to cover. Bring to a boil and boil hard for 15 minutes to remove any harmful toxins. Reduce the heat and simmer for 45 minutes.

2 Drain the beans and put into a clean saucepan with the water, ham bone, carrots, onion, celery, leek, bay leaves, and olive oil. Bring to a boil, then cover, and simmer for an hour or until the beans are very tender.

3 Discard the bay leaves and bone, reserving any ham pieces from the bone. Remove a small cupful of the beans and reserve. Purée or liquidize the soup in a food processor or blender, or push through a coarse strainer, and return to a clean pan.

4 Add the tomatoes, garlic, tomato paste, rice, and plenty of seasoning. Bring back to a boil and simmer for about 15 minutes or until the rice is tender.

5 Add the cabbage, reserved beans and ham, and continue to simmer for 5 minutes. Adjust the seasoning and serve very hot. If liked, a piece of toasted crusty bread may be put in the base of each soup bowl before ladling in the soup. If the soup is too thick, add a little boiling water or stock.

Step *2*

Step *4*

Step *5*

Cream of Artichoke Soup

*A creamy soup with the unique, subtle flavoring of Jerusalem artichokes
and a garnish of grated carrots for extra crunch.*

SERVES 4–6

INGREDIENTS

1½ lb Jerusalem artichokes
1 lemon, sliced thickly
¼ cup butter or margarine
2 onions, chopped
1 garlic clove, crushed
5½ cups chicken or
vegetable stock
2 bay leaves
¼ tsp ground mace or ground nutmeg
1 tbsp lemon juice
⅔ cup light cream or
natural fromage frais
salt and pepper

TO GARNISH

coarsely grated carrot
chopped fresh parsley or cilantro

1 Peel and slice the artichokes. Put into a bowl of water with the lemon slices.

2 Melt the butter or margarine in a large saucepan. Add the onions and garlic, and fry gently for 3–4 minutes until soft but not colored.

3 Drain the artichokes and add to the pan. Mix well and cook gently for 2–3 minutes without allowing to color.

4 Add the stock, seasoning, bay leaves, mace or nutmeg, and lemon juice. Bring slowly to a boil, then cover, and simmer gently for about 30 minutes until the vegetables are very tender.

5 Discard the bay leaves. Cool the soup slightly then press through a strainer or blend in a food processor until smooth. If liked, a little of the soup may be only partially puréed and added to the rest of the puréed soup, to give extra texture.

6 Pour into a clean pan and bring to a boil. Adjust the seasoning and stir in the cream or fromage frais. Reheat gently without boiling. Garnish with grated carrot and chopped parsley or cilantro.

Step *1*

Step *3*

Step *5*

Navy Bean & Pasta Soup

A dish with proud Mediterranean origins, this soup is a winter warmer, to be served with warm, crusty bread and, if you like, a slice of cheese.

SERVES 4

INGREDIENTS

generous 1 cup dried navy beans, soaked,
drained, and rinsed
4 tbsp olive oil
2 large onions, sliced
3 garlic cloves, chopped
14 oz can chopped tomatoes
1 tsp dried oregano
1 tsp tomato paste
3½ cups water
3 oz small pasta shapes, such as fusilli or
conchigliette
4 oz sun-dried tomatoes, drained
and sliced thinly
1 tbsp chopped cilantro or flat-leaf parsley
2 tbsp freshly grated Parmesan
salt and pepper

1 Put the soaked beans into a large pan, cover with cold water, and bring them to a boil. Boil rapidly for 15 minutes to remove any harmful toxins. Drain the beans in a colander.

2 Heat the oil in a pan over a medium heat and fry the onions until they are just beginning to change color. Stir in the garlic and cook for 1 further minute. Stir in the chopped tomatoes, oregano, and the tomato paste and pour on the water. Add the beans, bring to a boil, and cover the pan. Simmer for 45 minutes, or until the beans are almost tender.

3 Add the pasta, season the soup, and stir in the sun-dried tomatoes. Return the soup to a boil, partly cover the pan, and continue cooking for 10 minutes, or until the pasta is nearly tender.

4 Stir in the chopped cilantro or parsley. Taste the soup and adjust the seasoning if necessary. Transfer to a warm soup tureen to serve. Sprinkle with the cheese and serve hot.

Step *2*

Step *3*

Step *4*

Fish Soup

There are many varieties of fish soup in Italy, some including shellfish.
This one, from Tuscany, is more like a chowder.

SERVES 4-6

INGREDIENTS

2 lb assorted prepared fish (including
mixed fish fillets, squid, etc.)
2 onions, sliced thinly
2 celery stalks, sliced thinly
a few parsley sprigs
2 bay leaves
²⁄₃ cup white wine
4 cups water
2 tbsp olive oil
1 garlic clove, crushed
1 carrot, chopped finely
14 oz can peeled tomatoes, puréed
2 potatoes, chopped
1 tbsp tomato paste
1 tsp chopped fresh oregano or
½ tsp dried oregano
12 oz fresh mussels
6 oz peeled shrimp
2 tbsp chopped fresh parsley
salt and pepper
crusty bread, to serve

1 Cut the cleaned and prepared fish into slices or cubes and put into a large saucepan with half the onion and celery, the parsley sprigs, bay leaves, wine, and water. Bring to a boil, then cover, and simmer for about 25 minutes.

2 Strain the fish stock and discard the vegetables. Skin the fish, remove any bones, and reserve.

3 Heat the oil in a pan, finely chop the remaining onion, and fry with the garlic, carrot, and remaining celery until soft but not colored. Add the puréed canned tomatoes, potatoes, tomato paste, oregano, reserved stock, and seasonings. Bring to a boil and simmer for about 15 minutes or until the potato is almost tender.

4 Meanwhile, thoroughly scrub the mussels. Add to the pan with the shrimp and then simmer for about 5 minutes or until the mussels have opened (discard any that stay closed).

5 Return the fish to the soup with the chopped parsley, bring back to a boil, and simmer for 5 minutes. Adjust the seasoning.

6 Serve the soup in warm bowls with chunks of fresh crusty bread, or put a toasted slice of crusty bread in the bottom of each bowl before adding the soup. If possible, remove a few half shells from the mussels just before serving.

Step *1*

Step *4*

Step *5*

Mussels in White Wine

This soup of mussels cooked in white wine with onions and cream can be served as an appetizer or a main dish, with plenty of crusty bread.

SERVES 4

INGREDIENTS

12 cups fresh mussels
¼ cup butter
1 large onion, chopped very finely
2–3 garlic cloves, crushed
1½ cups dry white wine
⅔ cup water
2 tbsp lemon juice
good pinch of finely grated lemon rind
1 bouquet garni sachet
1 tbsp all-purpose flour
4 tbsp light or heavy cream
2–3 tbsp chopped fresh parsley
salt and pepper
warm crusty bread, to serve

1 Scrub the mussels in several changes of cold water to remove all mud, sand, barnacles, etc. Pull off all the "beards". All the mussels must be tightly closed; if they don't close when given a sharp tap, they must be discarded at once.

2 Melt half the butter in a large saucepan. Add the onion and garlic, and fry gently until soft but not colored.

3 Add the wine, water, lemon juice and rind, bouquet garni, and plenty of seasoning. Bring to a boil, then cover, and simmer for 4–5 minutes.

4 Add the mussels to the pan, cover tightly, and simmer for 5 minutes, shaking the pan frequently, until all the mussels have opened. Discard any mussels which have not opened. Remove the bouquet garni.

5 Remove the empty half shell from each mussel. Blend the remaining butter with the flour and beat into the soup, a little at a time. Simmer gently for 2–3 minutes until slightly thickened.

6 Add the cream and half the parsley to the soup and reheat gently. Adjust the seasoning. Ladle the mussels and soup into large warm soup bowls, sprinkle with the remaining parsley, and serve with warm crusty bread.

Step *1*

Step *3*

Step *5*

PASTA DISHES

The simplicity and satisfying nature of pasta in all its varieties makes it a universal favorite. Easy to cook and easy on the pocket, pasta is wonderfully versatile. It can be served in soups, with meat, fish, or vegetable sauces, or baked in the oven.

Some of the most popular and best-known pasta dishes are ones that combine long strands of pasta cooked "al dente", with a rich hearty meat sauce. Spaghetti Bolognese needs no introduction, and yet it is said that there are almost as many versions of this delicious regional dish as there are lovers of Italian food.

Fish and seafood are irresistible combined with pasta and need only the briefest of cooking times. Vermicelli with Clam Sauce (page 92), creamy Seafood Lasagne (page 100), and Pasta Shells with Mussels (page 90) will all give you a whiff of the sea, if not the Mediterranean.

Pasta combined with vegetables provides inspiration for countless dishes which will please vegetarians and meat-eaters alike.

Layered pasta dishes are perfect for parties, picnics, buffet meals, or informal dinners. Children and teenagers love them. Try Eggplant Cake (page 76) or Layered Meatloaf (page 74). They will make popular additions to your repertoire of baked pasta favorites.

Spaghetti Carbonara

Ensure all the cooked ingredients are as hot as possible, so that the beaten eggs are cooked on contact. It is a classic dish, to serve with a flourish.

SERVES 4

INGREDIENTS

14 oz spaghetti
2 tbsp olive oil
1 large onion, sliced thinly
2 garlic cloves, chopped
6 oz fatty bacon slices, rind removed, cut into thin strips
2 tbsp butter
6 oz mushrooms, sliced thinly
1¼ cups heavy cream
3 eggs, beaten
¾ cup grated Parmesan, plus extra to serve (optional)
freshly ground black pepper
sage sprigs, to garnish

1 Heat a large serving dish or bowl. Cook the spaghetti in a large pan of boiling salted water, adding 1 tablespoon of the oil. When the pasta is almost tender, drain in a colander. Return the spaghetti to the pan, cover, and leave it in a warm place.

2 While the spaghetti is cooking, heat the remaining oil in a skillet over a medium heat. Fry the onion until it is translucent, then add the garlic and bacon, and fry until the bacon is crisp.

3 Remove the onion, garlic, and bacon with a perforated spoon and set aside to keep warm. Heat the butter in the skillet and fry the mushrooms for 3–4 minutes, stirring them once or twice. Return the bacon mixture to the mushrooms. Cover and keep warm.

4 Stir together the cream, the beaten eggs, and cheese, and season with salt and pepper.

5 Working very quickly to avoid cooling the cooked ingredients, tip the spaghetti into the bacon and mushroom mixture and pour on the eggs. Toss the spaghetti quickly, using two forks, and serve it at once. If you wish, serve with extra grated Parmesan.

Step *3*

Step *4*

Step *5*

Tagliatelle with Chicken Sauce

*Spinach ribbon noodles covered with a rich tomato sauce and topped
with creamy chicken makes a very appetizing dish.*

SERVES 4

INGREDIENTS

Basic Tomato Sauce (page 13)
8 oz fresh green ribbon noodles
1 tbsp olive oil
salt
basil leaves, to garnish

CHICKEN SAUCE

¼ cup unsalted butter
14 oz boned, skinned chicken breast,
thinly sliced
¾ cup blanched almonds
1¼ cups heavy cream
salt and pepper
basil leaves, to garnish

1 Make the tomato sauce, and keep warm.

2 To make the chicken sauce, melt the butter in a pan over a medium heat and fry the chicken strips and almonds for 5–6 minutes, stirring frequently, until the chicken is cooked through.

3 Meanwhile, pour the cream into a small pan over a low heat, bring it to a boil, and boil for about 10 minutes, until reduced by almost half. Pour the cream over the chicken and almonds, stir well, and season. Set aside and keep warm.

4 Cook the pasta in a large pan of boiling salted water, first adding the oil. When the pasta is just tender, drain in a colander, then return it to the pan, cover, and keep warm.

5 Turn the pasta into a warm serving dish and spoon the tomato sauce over it. Spoon the chicken and cream over the center, scatter the basil leaves over, and serve at once.

Step *1*

Step *2*

Step *3*

Spaghetti Bolognese

This familiar meat sauce, known as ragù, may also be used in lasagne, and in other baked dishes. It can be made in large quantities and frozen.

SERVES 4

INGREDIENTS

14 oz spaghetti
1 tbsp olive oil
salt
1 tbsp butter
2 tbsp chopped fresh parsley, to garnish

RAGÙ

3 tbsp olive oil
3 tbsp butter
2 large onions, chopped
4 celery stalks, sliced thinly
6 oz fatty bacon, chopped into
small strips
2 garlic cloves, chopped
1 lb ground lean beef
2 tbsp tomato paste
1 tbsp flour
14 oz can chopped tomatoes
⅔ cup beef stock
⅔ cup red wine
2 tsp dried oregano
½ tsp freshly grated nutmeg
salt and pepper

1 To make the ragù: heat the oil and the butter in a large skillet over a medium heat. Add the onions, celery, and bacon pieces and fry them together for 5 minutes, stirring once or twice.

2 Stir in the garlic and ground beef and cook, stirring, until the meat has lost its redness. Lower the heat and continue cooking for a further 10 minutes, stirring once or twice.

3 Increase the heat to medium, stir in the tomato paste and the flour, and cook for 1–2 minutes. Stir in the chopped tomatoes, beef stock, and wine, and bring to a boil, stirring. Season the sauce and stir in the oregano and nutmeg. Cover the pan and simmer for 45 minutes, stirring occasionally.

4 Cook the spaghetti in a large pan of boiling salted water, adding the olive oil. When it is almost tender, drain in a colander, then return to the pan. Dot the spaghetti with the butter and toss thoroughly.

5 Taste the sauce and adjust the seasoning if necessary. Pour the sauce over the spaghetti and toss well. Sprinkle with the parsley and serve immediately.

Step *1*

Step *2*

Step *3*

Tagliatelle with Meatballs

*There is an appetizing contrast of textures and
flavors in this satisfying family dish.*

SERVES 4

INGREDIENTS

1 lb ground lean beef
1 cup soft white bread crumbs
1 garlic clove, crushed
2 tbsp chopped fresh parsley
1 tsp dried oregano
large pinch of freshly grated nutmeg
¼ tsp ground coriander
½ cup grated Parmesan
2–3 tbsp milk
flour, for dusting
4 tbsp olive oil
14 oz tagliatelle
2 tbsp butter, diced
salt
2 tbsp chopped fresh parsley, to garnish

SAUCE

3 tbsp olive oil
2 large onions, sliced
2 celery stalks, sliced thinly
2 garlic cloves, chopped
14 oz can chopped tomatoes
4 oz bottled sun-dried tomatoes,
drained and chopped
2 tbsp tomato paste
1 tbsp dark muscovado sugar
⅔ cup white wine, or water
salt and pepper
salad greens, to serve

1 To make the sauce, heat the oil in a skillet and fry the onion and celery until translucent. Add the garlic and cook for 1 minute. Stir in the tomatoes, tomato paste, sugar, and wine, and season. Bring to a boil and simmer for 10 minutes.

2 Break up the meat in a bowl with a wooden spoon until it becomes a sticky paste. Stir in the bread crumbs, garlic, herbs, and spices. Stir in the cheese and enough milk to make a firm paste. Flour your hands, take large spoonfuls of the mixture, and shape it into 12 balls. Heat the oil in a skillet and fry the meatballs for 5–6 minutes until browned.

3 Pour the tomato sauce over the meatballs. Lower the heat, cover the pan, and simmer for 30 minutes, turning once or twice. Add a little extra water if the sauce begins to dry.

4 Cook the pasta in a large saucepan of boiling salted water, adding the remaining oil. When almost tender, drain in a colander, then turn into a warm serving dish, dot with the butter, and toss with two forks. Spoon the meatballs and sauce over the pasta and sprinkle on the parsley. Serve with salad greens.

Step *1*

Step *2*

Step *3*

Lasagne Verde

*The sauce in this delicious baked pasta dish is the same sauce
that is served with Spaghetti Bolognese (page 66).*

SERVES 6

INGREDIENTS

Ragù (page 66)
1 tbsp olive oil
8 oz lasagne verde
½ cup Parmesan, grated
Béchamel Sauce (page 13)
salt and pepper
salad greens, tomato salad, or
black olives, to serve

1 Begin by making the ragù as described on page 66. Cook for 10–12 minutes longer than the time given, in an uncovered pan, to allow the excess liquid to evaporate. To layer the sauce with lasagne, it needs to be reduced to the consistency of a thick paste.

2 Have ready a large pan of boiling, salted water and add the olive oil. Drop the pasta sheets into the boiling water a few at a time, and return the water to a boil before adding further pasta sheets. If you are using fresh lasagne, cook the sheets for a total of 8 minutes. If you are using dried or partly pre-cooked pasta, cook it according to the directions given on the packet.

3 Remove the pasta sheets from the pan with a perforated spoon. Spread them in a single layer on damp dishcloths.

4 Grease a rectangular ovenproof dish, about 10–11 inches long. To assemble the dish, spoon a little of the meat sauce into the prepared dish, cover with a layer of lasagne, then spoon over a little béchamel sauce, and sprinkle some of the cheese. Continue making layers in this way, covering the final layer of lasagne with the remaining béchamel sauce.

5 Sprinkle on the remaining cheese and bake in a preheated oven, 375°F, for 40 minutes, until the sauce is golden brown and bubbling. Serve with salad greens, a tomato salad, or a bowl of black olives.

Step *2*

Step *3*

Step *4*

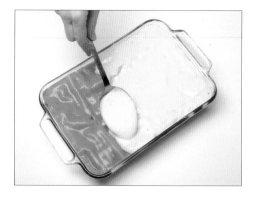

Stuffed Cannelloni

Cannelloni, the thick round pasta tubes, make perfect containers for close-textured sauces of all kinds.

SERVES 4

INGREDIENTS

8 cannelloni tubes
1 tbsp olive oil
fresh herb sprigs, to garnish

FILLING

2 tbsp butter
10 oz frozen spinach, defrosted
and chopped
½ cup Ricotta
¼ cup grated Parmesan
¼ cup chopped ham
¼ tsp freshly grated nutmeg
2 tbsp heavy cream
2 eggs, lightly beaten
salt and pepper

SAUCE

2 tbsp butter
¼ cup flour
1¼ cups milk
2 bay leaves
large pinch of grated nutmeg
¼ cup Parmesan, grated

1 To prepare the filling, melt the butter in a pan and stir in the spinach. Stir for 2–3 minutes to allow the moisture to evaporate, then remove the pan from the heat. Stir in the cheeses and the ham. Season with nutmeg, and salt and pepper. Beat in the cream and eggs to make a thick paste. Set aside to cool.

2 Cook the cannelloni in a large pan of boiling salted water, adding the olive oil. When almost tender, after 10–12 minutes, drain in a colander, and set aside to cool.

3 To make the sauce, melt the butter in a pan, stir in the flour and, when it has formed a roux, gradually pour on the milk, stirring all the time. Add the bay leaves, bring to simmering point, and cook for 5 minutes. Season with nutmeg, salt, and pepper. Remove the pan from the heat and discard the bay leaves.

4 To assemble the dish, spoon the filling into a piping bag and pipe it into each of the cannelloni tubes.

5 Spoon a little of the sauce into a shallow baking dish. Arrange the cannelloni in a single layer, then pour over the remaining sauce. Sprinkle on the remaining Parmesan cheese and bake in a preheated oven, 375°F, for 40–45 minutes, until the sauce is golden brown and bubbling. Serve garnished with fresh herb sprigs.

Step *2*

Step *4*

Step *5*

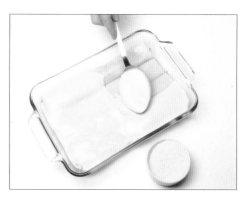

Layered Meatloaf

*The cheesy pasta layer comes as a pleasant surprise inside
this lightly spiced meatloaf.*

SERVES 6

INGREDIENTS

2 tbsp butter, plus extra for greasing
1 onion, chopped finely
1 small red bell pepper, cored, deseeded,
and chopped
1 garlic clove, chopped
1 lb ground lean beef
½ cup soft white bread crumbs
½ tsp cayenne pepper
1 tbsp lemon juice
½ tsp grated lemon rind
2 tbsp chopped fresh parsley
3 oz short pasta, such as fusilli
4 bay leaves
1 tbsp olive oil
Cheese Sauce (page 14)
6 oz fatty bacon slices, rind removed
salt and pepper
salad greens, to garnish

1 Melt the butter in a pan over a medium heat and fry the onion and pepper for about 3 minutes, until the onion is translucent. Stir in the garlic and cook for a further 1 minute.

2 Put the meat into a large bowl and mash it with a wooden spoon until it becomes a sticky paste. Tip in the fried vegetables and stir in the bread crumbs, cayenne, lemon juice, lemon rind, and parsley. Season the mixture with salt and pepper and set aside.

3 Cook the pasta in a large pan of boiling water to which you have added salt and the olive oil. When it is almost tender, drain in a colander. Stir the pasta into the cheese sauce.

4 Grease a 2 lb loaf pan and arrange the bay leaves in the base. Stretch the bacon slices with the back of a knife blade and arrange them to line the base and the sides of the pan.

5 Spoon in half the meat mixture, level the surface, and cover it with the pasta. Spoon in the remaining meat mixture, level the top, and cover the pan with foil.

6 Cook the meatloaf in a preheated oven, 350°F, for 1 hour, or until the juices run clear and the loaf has shrunk away from the sides of the pan. Pour off any excess fat from the pan and turn the loaf out onto a warm serving dish. Garnish with the salad greens and serve hot.

Step *4*

Step *5*

Step *6*

Eggplant Cake

Layers of toasty-brown eggplant, meat sauce, and cheese-flavored pasta make this a popular family supper dish.

SERVES 4

INGREDIENTS

1 eggplant, sliced thinly
5 tbsp olive oil
8 oz short pasta shapes, such as fusilli
¼ cup butter, plus extra for greasing
6 tbsp flour
1¼ cups milk
1⅔ cup light cream
⅔ cup chicken stock
large pinch of freshly grated nutmeg
¾ cup grated sharp hard cheese
¼ cup grated Parmesan
Lamb Sauce (page 13)
salt and pepper
artichoke heart and tomato salad, to serve

1 Put the eggplant slices in a colander, sprinkle with salt, and leave for about 45 minutes. Rinse under cold, running water and drain. Pat dry with paper towels.

2 Heat 4 tablespoons of the oil in a skillet over a medium heat. Fry the eggplant slices for about 4 minutes each side, until golden. Remove with a perforated spoon and drain on paper towels.

3 Meanwhile, cook the pasta in a large pan of boiling salted water, adding 1 tablespoon of olive oil. When the pasta is almost tender, drain it in a colander, and return to the pan. Cover and keep warm.

4 Melt the butter in a small pan, stir in the flour, and cook for 1 minute. Gradually pour in the milk, stirring all the time, then stir in the cream and chicken stock. Season with nutmeg, salt, and pepper, bring to a boil, and simmer for 5 minutes. Stir in the hard cheese and remove from the heat. Pour half the sauce over the pasta and mix well. Reserve the remaining sauce.

5 Grease a shallow ovenproof dish. Spoon in half the pasta, cover it with half the lamb sauce, and then with the eggplant in a single layer. Repeat the layers of pasta and lamb sauce and spread the remaining cheese sauce over the top. Sprinkle the Parmesan. Bake in a preheated oven, 375°F, for 25 minutes, until golden brown. Serve hot or cold, with artichoke heart and tomato salad.

Step *2*

Step *4*

Step *5*

Pasticcio

A recipe that has both Italian and Greek origins, this dish may be served hot or cold, cut into thick, satisfying squares.

SERVES 6

INGREDIENTS

8 oz fusilli, or other short pasta shapes
1 tbsp olive oil
4 tbsp heavy cream
salt
rosemary sprigs, to garnish

SAUCE

2 tbsp olive oil, plus extra for brushing
1 onion, sliced thinly
1 red bell pepper, cored, deseeded, and chopped
2 cloves garlic, chopped
1¼ lb ground lean beef
14 oz can chopped tomatoes
½ cup dry white wine
2 tbsp chopped fresh parsley
2 oz can anchovies, drained and chopped
salt and pepper

TOPPING

1¼ cups natural yogurt
3 eggs
pinch of freshly grated nutmeg
⅓ cup Parmesan, grated

1 To make the sauce, heat the oil in a large skillet and fry the onion and red bell pepper for 3 minutes. Stir in the garlic and cook for 1 minute more. Stir in the beef and cook, stirring frequently, until no longer pink.

2 Add the tomatoes and wine, stir well, and bring to a boil. Simmer, uncovered, for 20 minutes, until the sauce is fairly thick. Stir in the parsley and anchovies, and adjust the seasoning.

3 Cook the pasta in a large pan of boiling salted water, adding the oil. When almost tender, drain in a colander, then transfer to a bowl. Stir in the cream and set aside.

4 To make the topping, beat together the yogurt and eggs and season with nutmeg, salt, and pepper. Stir in the cheese.

5 Brush a shallow baking dish with oil. Spoon in half the macaroni and cover with half the meat sauce. Repeat these layers, spread the topping evenly over the dish, and sprinkle on the cheese.

6 Bake in a preheated oven, 375°F, for 25 minutes, until the topping is golden brown and bubbling. Garnish with rosemary sprigs and serve with a selection of raw vegetable crudités.

Step *1*

Step *4*

Step *5*

Tagliatelle with Pumpkin

This unusual pasta dish comes from the Emilia Romagna region.

SERVES 4

INGREDIENTS

1 lb pumpkin or butternut squash
2 tbsp olive oil
1 onion, chopped finely
2 garlic cloves, crushed
4–6 tbsp chopped fresh parsley
good pinch of ground or freshly grated nutmeg
about 1 cup chicken or vegetable stock
4 oz prosciutto, cut into narrow strips
9 oz tagliatelle, green or white (fresh or dried)
⅔ cup heavy cream
salt and pepper
freshly grated Parmesan, to serve

1 Peel the pumpkin or butternut squash and scoop out the seeds and membrane. Cut the flesh into ½ in. dice.

2 Heat the oil in a pan and gently fry the onion and garlic until soft. Add half the parsley and fry for a minute or so longer.

3 Add the pumpkin or squash and continue to cook for 2–3 minutes. Season well with salt, pepper, and nutmeg. Add half the stock, bring to a boil, cover, and simmer for about 10 minutes or until the pumpkin is tender, adding more stock as necessary. Add the prosciutto and continue to cook for a further 2 minutes, stirring frequently.

4 Meanwhile, cook the tagliatelle in a large saucepan of boiling salted water, allowing 3–4 minutes for fresh pasta or about 12 minutes for dried (or follow the directions on the packet). When tender but still with some bite, drain thoroughly, and turn into a warm dish.

5 Add the cream to the ham mixture and heat gently until really hot. Adjust the seasoning and spoon over the pasta. Sprinkle with the remaining parsley and hand the grated Parmesan separately.

Step *1*

Step *2*

Step *3*

Tortellini

*According to legend, the shape of the tortellini resembles Venus's navel.
When you make tortellini you will know what they should look like!*

SERVES 4

INGREDIENTS

FILLING

4 oz boned and skinned chicken breast
2 oz prosciutto
1½ oz cooked spinach, well drained
1 tbsp finely chopped onion
2 tbsp freshly grated Parmesan
good pinch of ground allspice
1 egg, beaten
salt and pepper
Basic Pasta Dough (page 11)

SAUCE

1¼ cups light cream
1–2 garlic cloves, crushed
4 oz button mushrooms, sliced thinly
4 tbsp freshly grated Parmesan
1–2 tbsp chopped fresh parsley

1 Poach the chicken in well-seasoned water until tender, about 10 minutes; drain and chop roughly. When cool put into a food processor with the prosciutto, spinach, and onion and process until finely chopped. Stir in the Parmesan, allspice, seasonings, and egg.

2 Roll out the pasta dough, half at a time, on a lightly floured counter until as thin as possible. Cut into 1½–2 in. rounds using a plain cutter.

3 Place ½ teaspoon of the filling in the center of each dough round, fold the pieces in half to make a semi-circle, and press the edges firmly together. Wrap the semi-circle around your index finger and cross over the two ends, pressing firmly together, curling the rest of the dough backward to make a navel shape. Slip the tortellini off your finger and lay on a lightly floured tray. Repeat with the rest of the dough, re-rolling the trimmings.

4 Heat a large pan of salted boiling water and add a few tortellini. Bring back to a boil and once they rise to the surface cook for about 5 minutes, giving an occasional stir. Remove with a perforated spoon and drain on paper towels. Keep warm in a dish while cooking the remainder.

5 To make the sauce, heat the cream with the garlic in a pan and bring to a boil. Simmer for a few minutes. Add the mushrooms, half the Parmesan, and seasoning and simmer for 2–3 minutes. Stir in the parsley and pour over the warm tortellini. Sprinkle the tortellini with the remaining Parmesan and serve immediately.

Step *3*

Step *3*

Step *4*

Sicilian Spaghetti

This delicious Sicilian dish originated as a handy way of using up leftover cooked pasta. Any variety of long pasta could be used.

SERVES 4

INGREDIENTS

2 eggplants, about 1¼ lb
⅔ cup olive oil
12 oz finely ground lean beef
1 onion, chopped
2 garlic cloves, crushed
2 tbsp tomato paste
14 oz can chopped tomatoes
1 tsp Worcestershire sauce
1 tsp chopped fresh oregano or marjoram
or ½ tsp dried oregano or marjoram
1½ oz pitted black olives, sliced
1 green, red, or yellow bell pepper, cored,
deseeded, and chopped
6 oz spaghetti
1 cup grated Parmesan
salt and pepper
fresh oregano or parsley, to garnish (optional)

1 Brush an 8 in. loose-based round cake pan with olive oil, place a round of baking parchment in the base, and brush with oil. Trim the eggplant and cut into slanting slices, ¼ in. thick. Heat some of the oil in a skillet. Fry a few slices at a time until lightly browned, turning once, and adding more oil as necessary. Drain on paper towels.

2 Put the ground beef, onion, and garlic into a saucepan and cook, stirring frequently, until browned all over. Add the tomato paste, tomatoes, Worcestershire sauce, herbs, and seasoning. Simmer for 10 minutes, stirring occasionally, then add the olives and bell pepper, and cook for a further 10 minutes.

3 Bring a large pan of salted water to a boil. Cook the spaghetti for 12–14 minutes until just tender. Drain thoroughly. Turn the spaghetti into a bowl and mix in the meat mixture and Parmesan, tossing with two forks.

4 Lay overlapping slices of eggplant evenly over the base of the cake pan and up the sides. Add the meat mixture, pressing it down, and cover with the remaining slices of eggplant.

5 Stand in a roasting pan and cook in a preheated oven, 400°F, for 40 minutes. Leave to stand for 5 minutes, then loosen around the edges and invert onto a warm serving dish, releasing the pan clip. Remove the parchment. Sprinkle with herbs before serving, if liked. Serve with extra Parmesan, if liked.

Step *1*

Step *3*

Step *4*

Spaghetti with Seafood Sauce

Frozen shelled shrimp from the freezer can become the star ingredient in this colorful and tasty dish.

SERVES 4

INGREDIENTS

8 oz short-cut spaghetti, or long
spaghetti broken into 6 in. lengths
2 tbsp olive oil
1¼ cups chicken stock
1 tsp lemon juice
1 small cauliflower, cut into flowerets
2 carrots, sliced thinly
4 oz snow peas, trimmed
¼ cup butter
1 onion, sliced
8 oz zucchini, sliced thinly
1 garlic clove, chopped
12 oz frozen shelled shrimp, defrosted
2 tbsp chopped fresh parsley
¼ cup grated Parmesan
salt and pepper
½ tsp paprika, to sprinkle
4 unshelled shrimp, to garnish (optional)

1 Cook the spaghetti in a large pan of boiling salted water, adding 1 tablespoon of the olive oil. When almost tender, drain, then return to the pan, and stir in the remaining olive oil. Cover and keep warm.

2 Bring the chicken stock and lemon juice to a boil. Add the cauliflower and carrots and cook for 3–4 minutes until they are barely tender. Remove with a perforated spoon and set aside. Add the snow peas and cook for 1–2 minutes, until they begin to soften. Remove with a perforated spoon and add to the other vegetables. Reserve the stock for future use.

3 Melt half the butter in a skillet over medium heat and fry the onion and zucchini for about 3 minutes. Add the garlic and shrimp and cook for a further 2–3 minutes until thoroughly heated through.

4 Stir in the reserved vegetables and heat through. Season well, then stir in the remaining butter.

5 Transfer the spaghetti to a warm serving dish. Pour on the sauce and parsley. Toss well using two forks, until thoroughly coated. Sprinkle on the grated cheese and paprika, and garnish with unshelled shrimp, if using. Serve immediately.

Step *2*

Step *3*

Step *4*

Steamed Pasta Pudding

A tasty mixture of creamy fish and pasta cooked in a bowl, unmolded,
and drizzled with tomato sauce presents macaroni in a new guise.

SERVES 4

INGREDIENTS

4 oz short-cut macaroni, or other
short pasta shapes
1 tbsp olive oil
1 tbsp butter, plus extra for greasing
1 lb white fish fillets, such as cod
or haddock
a few parsley stalks
6 black peppercorns
½ cup heavy cream
2 eggs, separated
2 tbsp chopped fresh dill, or parsley
freshly ground black pepper
pinch of freshly grated nutmeg
½ cup grated Parmesan
Basic Tomato Sauce (page 13), to serve
dill or parsley sprigs, to garnish

1 Cook the pasta in a large pan of salted boiling water, adding the oil. Drain in a colander, return to the pan, add the butter, and cover the pan. Keep warm.

2 Place the fish in a skillet with the parsley stalks, peppercorns, and just enough water to cover. Bring to a boil, cover, and simmer for 10 minutes. Lift out the fish with a slice, reserving the liquor. When the fish is cool enough to handle, skin, and remove any remaining bones. Cut into bite-size pieces.

3 Transfer the pasta to a large bowl and stir in the cream, egg yolks, and dill. Stir in the fish, taking care not to break it up, and enough liquor to make a moist but firm mixture. It should fall easily from a spoon but not be too runny. Whip the egg whites until stiff but not dry, then fold into the mixture.

4 Grease a heatproof bowl and spoon in the mixture to within 1½ inches of the rim. Cover the top with greased baking parchment and a cloth, or with foil, and tie firmly around the rim. Do not use foil if you cook the pudding in a microwave.

5 Stand the pudding on a trivet in a large pan of boiling water to come halfway up the sides. Cover and steam for 1½ hours, topping up the boiling water as needed, or cook in a microwave on maximum power for 7 minutes.

6 Run a knife around the inside of the bowl and invert onto a warm serving dish. Pour some tomato sauce over the top and serve the rest separately. Garnish with the herb sprigs.

Step *2*

Step *3*

Step *5*

Pasta Shells with Mussels

*Serve this aromatic seafood dish to family and friends
who admit to a love of garlic.*

SERVES 4–6

INGREDIENTS

14 oz pasta shells
1 tbsp olive oil

SAUCE

6 pints mussels, scrubbed
1 cup dry white wine
2 large onions, chopped
½ cup unsalted butter
6 large garlic cloves, chopped finely
5 tbsp chopped fresh parsley
1¼ cups heavy cream
salt and pepper
crusty bread, to serve

1 Pull off the "beards" from the mussels and rinse well in several changes of water. Discard any mussels that refuse to close when tapped. Put the mussels in a large pan with the white wine and half the onions. Cover the pan, shake, and cook over a medium heat for 2–3 minutes until the mussels open.

2 Remove the pan from the heat, lift out the mussels with a perforated spoon, reserving the liquor, and set aside until they are cool enough to handle. Discard any mussels that have not opened.

3 Melt the butter in a pan over medium heat and fry the remaining onion until translucent. Stir in the garlic and cook for 1 minute more. Gradually pour on the reserved cooking liquor, stirring to blend thoroughly. Stir in the parsley and cream. Season and bring to simmering point. Taste and adjust the seasoning if necessary.

4 Cook the pasta in a large pan of salted boiling water, adding the oil. When it is almost tender, drain in a colander. Return to the pan, cover, and keep warm.

5 Remove the mussels from their shells, reserving a few shells for garnish. Stir the mussels into the cream sauce. Tip the pasta into a warm serving dish, pour on the sauce, and, using two large spoons, toss it well. Garnish with a few mussel shells. Serve hot, with warm bread.

Step 2

Step 3

Step 5

Vermicelli with Clam Sauce

*A quickly cooked recipe that transforms store-cupboard ingredients
into a dish with style.*

SERVES 4

INGREDIENTS

14 oz vermicelli, spaghetti, or
other long pasta
1 tbsp olive oil
2 tbsp butter
2 tbsp Parmesan shavings, to garnish
basil sprig, to garnish

SAUCE

1 tbsp olive oil
2 onions, chopped
2 garlic cloves, chopped
2 × 7 oz jars clams in brine
½ cup white wine
4 tbsp chopped fresh parsley
½ tsp dried oregano
pinch of freshly grated nutmeg
salt and pepper

1 Cook the pasta in a large pan of boiling salted water, adding the olive oil. When it is almost tender, drain in a colander, return to the pan, and add the butter. Cover the pan. Shake it and keep it warm.

2 To make the clam sauce, heat the oil in a pan over a medium heat and fry the onion until it is translucent. Stir in the garlic and cook for 1 further minute.

3 Strain the liquid from one jar of clams, pour into the pan, and add the wine. Stir well, bring to simmering point, and simmer for 3 minutes. Drain the brine from the second jar of clams and discard.

4 Add the shellfish and herbs to the pan, and season with pepper and nutmeg. Lower the heat and cook until the sauce is heated through.

5 Transfer the pasta to a warm serving dish and pour on the sauce. Sprinkle with the Parmesan and garnish with the basil sprig. Serve hot.

Step *2*

Step *3*

Step *4*

Spaghetti with Smoked Salmon

*Made in moments, this is a dish to astonish and delight
unexpected guests.*

SERVES 4

INGREDIENTS

1 lb buckwheat spaghetti
2 tbsp olive oil
½ cup crumbled feta cheese
cilantro or parsley, to garnish

SAUCE

1¼ cups heavy cream
⅔ cup whiskey or brandy
4 oz smoked salmon
large pinch of cayenne pepper
2 tbsp chopped cilantro or parsley
salt and pepper

1 Cook the spaghetti in a large pan of salted boiling water, adding 1 tablespoon of the olive oil. When the pasta is almost tender, drain in a colander. Return to the pan and sprinkle on the remaining oil. Cover, shake the pan, and keep warm.

2 In separate small pans, heat the cream and the whiskey or brandy to simmering point. Do not let them boil.

3 Combine the cream with the whiskey or brandy. Cut the smoked salmon into thin strips and add to the cream mixture. Season with pepper and cayenne, and stir in the cilantro or parsley.

4 Transfer the spaghetti to a warm serving dish, pour on the sauce, and toss thoroughly using two large forks. Scatter the crumbled cheese over the pasta and garnish with the cilantro or parsley. Serve at once.

Step *1*

Step *2*

Step *3*

Spaghetti with Tuna & Parsley Sauce

*This is a recipe to look forward to when parsley is at its most prolific,
in the growing season.*

SERVES 4

INGREDIENTS

1 lb spaghetti
1 tbsp olive oil
2 tbsp butter
black olives, to garnish

SAUCE

7 oz can tuna, drained
2 oz can anchovies, drained
1 cup olive oil
1 cup roughly chopped fresh, flat-leaf parsley
⅔ cup crème fraîche
salt and pepper

1 Cook the spaghetti in a large pan of salted boiling water, adding the olive oil. When almost tender, drain in a colander, and return to the pan. Add the butter, toss thoroughly to coat, and keep warm.

2 Remove any bones from the tuna. Put it into a blender or food processor with the anchovies, olive oil, and parsley and process until the sauce is smooth. Pour in the crème fraîche and process for a few seconds to blend. Taste the sauce and season.

3 Warm 4 plates. Shake the pan of spaghetti over medium heat until it is thoroughly warmed through.

4 Pour on the sauce and toss quickly, using two forks. Garnish with the olives and serve immediately with warm, crusty bread.

Step *2*

Step *3*

Step *4*

Macaroni & Shrimp Bake

*This adaptation of an 18th-century Italian dish is baked until it is golden
brown and sizzling, then cut into wedges, like a cake.*

SERVES 4

INGREDIENTS

12 oz short pasta, such as
short-cut macaroni
1 tbsp olive oil, plus extra for brushing
6 tbsp butter, plus extra for greasing
2 small fennel bulbs, sliced thinly,
leaves reserved
6 oz mushrooms, sliced thinly
6 oz shelled shrimp
½ cup Parmesan, grated
2 large tomatoes, sliced
1 tsp dried oregano
salt and pepper
pinch of cayenne
Béchamel Sauce (page 13)

1 Cook the pasta in a large pan of boiling, salted water with 1 tablespoon of olive oil. When almost tender, drain the pasta in a colander, return to the pan, and dot with 2 tablespoons of the butter. Shake the pan well, cover, and keep warm.

2 Melt the remaining butter in a pan over medium heat and fry the fennel for 3–4 minutes, until it begins to soften. Stir in the mushrooms and fry for a further 2 minutes. Stir in the shrimp, remove the pan from the heat, and set aside.

3 Make the béchamel sauce and add the cayenne. Remove the pan from the heat and stir in the reserved vegetables, shrimp, and the pasta.

4 Grease a round, shallow baking dish. Pour in the pasta mixture and spread evenly. Sprinkle on the Parmesan, and arrange the tomato slices in a ring around the edge of the dish. Brush the tomato with olive oil and sprinkle on the dried oregano.

5 Bake in a preheated oven, 350°F, for 25 minutes, until golden brown. Serve hot.

Step *2*

Step *3*

Step *4*

Seafood Lasagne

Layers of cheese sauce, smoked cod, and whole wheat lasagne can be assembled overnight and left ready to cook on the following day.

SERVES 6

INGREDIENTS

8 sheets whole wheat lasagne
1 lb smoked cod
2½ cups milk
1 tbsp lemon juice
8 peppercorns
2 bay leaves
a few parsley stalks
½ cup grated sharp hard cheese
¼ cup grated Parmesan
salt and pepper
a few whole shrimp, to garnish (optional)

SAUCE

¼ cup butter, plus extra for greasing
1 large onion, sliced
1 green bell pepper, cored, deseeded, and chopped
1 small zucchini, sliced
½ cup flour
⅔ cup white wine
⅔ cup light cream
4 oz shelled shrimp
½ cup grated sharp hard cheese

1 Cook the lasagne in boiling, salted water until almost tender, as described on page 70. Drain and reserve.

2 Place the smoked cod, milk, lemon juice, peppercorns, bay leaves, and parsley stalks in a skillet. Bring to a boil, cover, and simmer for 10 minutes.

3 Lift the fish from the skillet with a perforated spoon. Remove the skin and any bones. Flake the fish. Strain and reserve the liquor.

4 Make the sauce: melt the butter in a pan and fry the onion, bell pepper, and zucchini for 2–3 minutes. Stir in the flour and cook for 1 minute. Gradually add the fish liquor, then stir in the wine, cream, and shrimp. Simmer for 2 minutes. Remove from the heat, add the cheese, and season well.

5 Grease a shallow baking dish. Pour in a fourth of the sauce and spread evenly over the base. Cover the sauce with three sheets of lasagne, then with another fourth of the sauce.

6 Arrange the fish on top, then cover with half the remaining sauce. Finish with the remaining lasagne, then the rest of the sauce. Sprinkle the hard cheese and Parmesan over the sauce.

7 Bake in a preheated oven, 375°F, for 25 minutes, or until the top is golden brown and bubbling. Garnish with a few whole shrimp, if liked.

Step *2*

Step *5*

Step *6*

Squid & Macaroni Stew

This seafood dish is quick and easy to make, yet is deliciously satisfying to eat.

SERVES 4–6

INGREDIENTS

8 oz short-cut macaroni, or other
short pasta shapes
1 tbsp olive oil
2 tbsp chopped fresh parsley
salt and pepper

SAUCE

12 oz cleaned squid, cut into ½ in. strips
6 tbsp olive oil
2 onions, sliced
1 cup fish stock
⅔ cup red wine
12 oz tomatoes, peeled and
thinly sliced
2 tbsp tomato paste
1 tsp dried oregano
2 bay leaves

1 Cook the pasta for only 3 minutes in a large pan of boiling salted water, adding the oil. Drain in a colander, return to the pan, cover, and keep warm.

2 To make the sauce, heat the oil in a pan over medium heat and fry the onion until translucent. Add the squid and stock and simmer for 5 minutes. Pour on the wine and add the tomatoes, tomato paste, oregano, and bay leaves. Bring the sauce to a boil, season, and cook, uncovered, for 5 minutes.

3 Add the pasta, stir well, cover the pan, and continue simmering it for 10 minutes, or until the macaroni and squid are almost tender. By this time the sauce should be thick and syrupy. If it is too liquid, uncover the pan and continue cooking for a few minutes. Taste the sauce and adjust the seasoning if necessary.

4 Remove the bay leaves and stir in most of the parsley, reserving a little to garnish. Transfer to a warm serving dish. Sprinkle on the remaining parsley and serve hot. Serve with warm, crusty Italian bread.

Step *2*

Step *3*

Step *4*

Green Garlic Tagliatelle

A rich pasta dish for garlic lovers everywhere. It's quick and easy to prepare and full of flavor.

SERVES 4

INGREDIENTS

2 tbsp walnut oil
1 bunch scallions, sliced
2 garlic cloves, sliced thinly
8 oz mushrooms, sliced
1 lb fresh green and white tagliatelle
8 oz frozen chopped leaf spinach, thawed and drained
½ cup full-fat soft cheese with garlic and herbs
4 tbsp light cream
½ cup chopped, unsalted pistachio nuts
2 tbsp shredded fresh basil
salt and pepper
fresh basil sprigs, to garnish
Italian bread, to serve

1 Gently heat the oil in a wok or skillet and fry the scallions and garlic for 1 minute until just softened. Add the mushrooms, stir well, cover, and cook gently for 5 minutes until softened.

2 Meanwhile, bring a large saucepan of lightly salted water to a boil and cook the pasta for 3–5 minutes until just tender. Drain well and return to the saucepan.

3 Add the spinach to the mushrooms and heat through for 1–2 minutes. Add the cheese and allow to melt slightly. Stir in the cream and continue to heat without allowing to boil.

4 Pour over the pasta, season, and mix well. Heat gently, stirring, for 2–3 minutes.

5 Pile into a warmed serving bowl and sprinkle over the pistachio nuts and shredded basil. Garnish with basil sprigs and serve with Italian bread.

Step *1*

Step *3*

Step *4*

Baked Eggplant with Pasta

Combined with tomatoes and Mozzarella, pasta makes a tasty filling for baked eggplant shells.

SERVES 4

INGREDIENTS

8 oz penne, or other short
pasta shapes
4 tbsp olive oil, plus extra for brushing
2 eggplants
1 large onion, chopped
2 garlic cloves, crushed
14 oz can chopped tomatoes
2 tsp dried oregano
2 oz Mozzarella, thinly sliced
¼ cup grated Parmesan
2 tbsp dry bread crumbs
salt and pepper
salad greens, to serve

1 Cook the pasta in a large pan of salted boiling water, adding 1 tablespoon of the olive oil. When it is almost tender, drain the pasta in a colander, return to the pan, cover, and keep warm.

2 Cut the eggplants in half lengthwise. Score around the inside with a knife, then scoop out the flesh with a spoon, taking care not to pierce the skin. Brush the insides of the eggplant shells with olive oil. Chop the flesh and set it aside.

3 Heat the remaining oil in a skillet over a medium heat and fry the onion until it is translucent. Add the garlic and fry for 1 further minute. Add the chopped eggplant and fry for 5 minutes, stirring frequently. Add the tomatoes and oregano, and season with salt and pepper. Bring to a boil and simmer for 10 minutes, or until the mixture is thick. Taste and adjust the seasoning if necessary. Remove from the heat and stir in the reserved pasta.

4 Brush a cookie sheet with oil and arrange the eggplant shells in a single layer. Divide half the tomato mixture between the 4 shells. Arrange the Mozzarella on top and cover with the remaining mixture, piling it into a mound. Mix together the Parmesan and bread crumbs, and sprinkle over the top, patting it lightly into the mixture.

5 Bake in a preheated oven, 400°F, for 25 minutes, until the topping is golden. Serve hot, with salad greens.

Step *2*

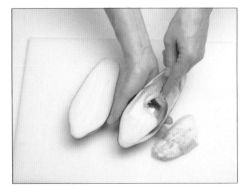

Step *3*

Step *4*

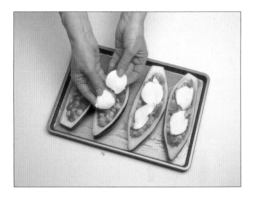

Mediterranean Spaghetti

Delicious Mediterranean vegetables, cooked in a rich tomato sauce, make an ideal topping for nutty whole wheat pasta.

SERVES 4

INGREDIENTS

2 tbsp olive oil
1 large red onion, chopped
2 garlic cloves, crushed
1 tbsp lemon juice
4 baby eggplants, quartered
2½ cups strained tomatoes (passata)
2 tsp superfine sugar
2 tbsp tomato paste
14 oz can artichoke hearts, drained
and halved
¾ cup pitted black olives
12 oz whole wheat dried spaghetti
salt and pepper
fresh basil sprigs, to garnish
olive bread, to serve

1 Heat 1 tablespoon of the oil in a large skillet and gently fry the onion, garlic, lemon juice, and eggplants for 4–5 minutes until lightly browned.

2 Pour in the strained tomatoes, season, and add the sugar and tomato paste. Bring to a boil, reduce the heat, and simmer for 20 minutes.

3 Gently stir in the artichoke halves and olives and cook for 5 minutes.

4 Meanwhile, bring a large saucepan of lightly salted water to a boil, and cook the spaghetti for 7–8 minutes until just tender. Drain well, toss in the remaining olive oil, and season.

5 Pile into a warm serving bowl and top with the vegetable sauce. Garnish with basil sprigs and serve with olive bread.

Step *1*

Step *2*

Step *3*

Zucchini & Eggplant Lasagne

This rich, baked pasta dish is packed full of vegetables, tomatoes, and Italian Mozzarella cheese.

SERVES 6

INGREDIENTS

2 lb eggplant
4 tbsp salt
8 tbsp olive oil
2 tbsp garlic and herb butter
or margarine
1 lb zucchini, sliced
2 cups grated Mozzarella
2½ cups strained tomatoes (passata)
6 sheets pre-cooked green lasagne
2½ cups Béchamel Sauce
(page 13)
½ cup grated Parmesan
1 tsp dried oregano
black pepper

1 Thinly slice the eggplant. Layer the slices in a bowl, sprinkling with the salt as you go. Set aside for 30 minutes. Rinse well in cold water and pat dry with paper towels.

2 Heat 4 tablespoons of the oil in a large skillet until very hot and gently fry half the eggplant slices for 6–7 minutes until lightly golden all over. Drain on paper towels. Repeat with the remaining eggplant slices and oil.

3 Melt the garlic and herb butter or margarine in the skillet and fry the zucchini for 5–6 minutes until golden. Drain on paper towels.

4 Place half the eggplant and zucchini slices in a large ovenproof dish. Season with pepper and sprinkle over half the Mozzarella. Spoon over half the strained tomatoes (passata) and top with three sheets of lasagne.

5 Arrange the remaining eggplant and zucchini slices on top. Season with pepper and top with the remaining Mozzarella and strained tomatoes (passata), and another layer of lasagne.

6 Spoon over the béchamel sauce and top with Parmesan and oregano. Put on a cookie sheet and bake in a preheated oven, 425°F, for 30–35 minutes until golden brown.

Step *3*

Step *5*

Step *6*

Tricolor Timballini

An unusual way of serving pasta, these cheesy molds are excellent served
with a crunchy salad for a light lunch.

SERVES 4

INGREDIENTS

1 tbsp butter or margarine, softened
½ cup dried white bread crumbs
6 oz tricolor spaghetti
1¼ cups Béchamel Sauce
(page 13)
1 egg yolk
1 cup grated Swiss cheese
salt and pepper
fresh flat-leaf parsley, to garnish

SAUCE

2 tsp olive oil
1 onion, chopped finely
1 bay leaf
⅔ cup dry white wine
⅔ cup strained tomatoes (passata)
1 tbsp tomato paste

1 Grease four ¾ cup molds or ramekins with the butter or margarine. Evenly coat the insides with half the bread crumbs.

2 Break the spaghetti into 2 in. lengths. Bring a saucepan of lightly salted water to a boil and cook the spaghetti for 5–6 minutes until just tender. Drain well and put in a bowl.

3 Mix the béchamel sauce, egg yolk, cheese, and seasoning into the cooked pasta and pack into the molds or ramekins.

4 Sprinkle with the remaining bread crumbs and put on a cookie sheet. Bake in a preheated oven, 425°F, for 20 minutes until golden. Leave to stand for 10 minutes.

5 Meanwhile, make the sauce. Heat the oil in a saucepan and gently fry the onion and bay leaf for 2–3 minutes until just softened.

6 Stir in the wine, strained tomatoes (passata), tomato paste, and seasoning. Bring to a boil and simmer for 20 minutes until thickened. Discard the bay leaf.

7 Run a spatula around the inside of the molds or ramekins. Turn onto serving plates, garnish, and serve with the tomato sauce.

Step *2*

Step *3*

Step *4*

Vegetable Pasta Stir-Fry

*Prepare all the vegetables and cook the pasta in advance,
then the dish can be cooked in a few minutes.*

SERVES 4

INGREDIENTS

14 oz whole wheat pasta shells, or other
short pasta shapes
1 tbsp olive oil
2 carrots, sliced thinly
4 oz baby corncobs
3 tbsp peanut oil
1-in. piece ginger root, sliced thinly
1 large onion, sliced thinly
1 garlic clove, sliced thinly
3 celery stalks, sliced thinly
1 small red bell pepper, cored, deseeded, and
sliced into matchstick strips
1 small green bell pepper, cored, deseeded,
and sliced into matchstick strips
salt
steamed snow peas, to serve

SAUCE

1 tsp cornstarch
2 tbsp water
3 tbsp soy sauce
3 tbsp dry sherry
1 tsp clear honey
few drops of hot pepper sauce (optional)

1 Cook the pasta in a large pan of boiling salted water, adding the tablespoon of olive oil. When almost tender, drain the pasta in a colander, return to the pan, cover, and keep warm.

2 Cook the carrots and corncobs in boiling, salted water for 2 minutes. Drain in a colander, plunge into cold water to prevent further cooking, and drain again.

3 Heat the peanut oil in a wok or large skillet over medium heat and fry the ginger for 1 minute, to flavor the oil. Remove with a slotted spoon and discard.

4 Add the onion, garlic, celery, and bell peppers to the oil and stir-fry for 2 minutes. Add the carrots and corncobs, and stir-fry for a further 2 minutes, then stir in the reserved pasta.

5 Put the cornstarch in a small bowl and mix to a smooth paste with the water. Stir in the soy sauce, sherry, and honey.

6 Pour the sauce into the pan, stir well, and cook for 2 minutes, stirring once or twice. Taste the sauce and season with hot pepper sauce if liked. Serve with a steamed green vegetable, such as snow peas.

Step *3*

Step *4*

Step *6*

Pasta with Green Vegetable Sauce

The different shapes and textures of the vegetables make a mouthwatering presentation in this light and summery dish.

SERVES 4

INGREDIENTS

8 oz gemelli or other pasta shapes
1 tbsp olive oil
2 tbsp chopped fresh parsley
2 tbsp freshly grated Parmesan
salt and pepper

SAUCE

1 head green broccoli, cut into flowerets
2 zucchini, sliced
8 oz asparagus spears, trimmed
4 oz snow peas, trimmed
4 oz frozen peas
2 tbsp butter
3 tbsp vegetable stock
5 tbsp heavy cream
large pinch of freshly grated nutmeg

1 Cook the pasta in a large pan of salted boiling water, adding the olive oil. When almost tender, drain in a colander, return to the pan, cover, and keep warm.

2 Steam the broccoli, zucchini, asparagus spears, and snow peas over a pan of boiling, salted water until just beginning to soften. Remove from the heat and plunge into cold water to prevent further cooking. Drain and set aside.

3 Cook the peas in boiling, salted water for 3 minutes, then drain. Refresh in cold water and drain again.

4 Put the butter and vegetable stock in a pan over a medium heat. Add all the vegetables, except the asparagus spears, and toss carefully with a wooden spoon to heat through, taking care not to break them up.

5 Stir in the cream, allow the sauce just to heat through, and season with salt, pepper, and nutmeg.

6 Transfer the pasta to a warm serving dish and stir in the chopped parsley. Spoon the sauce over, and sprinkle on the Parmesan. Arrange the asparagus spears in a pattern on top. Serve hot.

Step *2*

Step *4*

Step *5*

Vegetarian Pasta & Bean Casserole

A satisfying winter dish, this vegetable, pasta, and bean casserole with a crunchy topping is a slow-cooked, one-pot meal.

SERVES 6

INGREDIENTS

generous 1 cup dried navy beans,
soaked overnight and drained
8 oz penne, or other short pasta shapes
6 tbsp olive oil
3½ cups vegetable stock
2 large onions, sliced
2 cloves garlic, chopped
2 bay leaves
1 tsp dried oregano
1 tsp dried thyme
5 tbsp red wine
2 tbsp tomato paste
2 celery stalks, sliced
1 fennel bulb, sliced
4 oz mushrooms, sliced
8 oz tomatoes, sliced
1 tsp dark muscovado sugar
4 tbsp dry white bread crumbs
salt and pepper

TO SERVE

salad greens
crusty bread

1 Put the beans in a large pan, cover them with water, and bring to a boil. Boil the beans rapidly for 20 minutes, then drain them.

2 Cook the pasta for only 3 minutes in a large pan of boiling salted water, adding 1 tablespoon of the oil. Drain in a colander and set aside.

3 Put the beans in a large flameproof casserole, pour on the vegetable stock, and stir in the remaining olive oil, the onions, garlic, bay leaves, herbs, wine, and tomato paste.

4 Bring to a boil, cover the casserole, and cook in a preheated oven, 350°F, for 2 hours.

5 Add the reserved pasta, the celery, fennel, mushrooms, and tomatoes, and season with salt and pepper.

6 Stir in the sugar and sprinkle on the bread crumbs. Cover the casserole and continue cooking for another hour. Serve hot, with salad greens and plenty of crusty bread.

Step *3*

Step *5*

Step *6*

Vermicelli Flan

*Lightly cooked vermicelli is pressed into a flan ring and baked
with a creamy mushroom filling.*

SERVES 4

INGREDIENTS

8 oz vermicelli or spaghetti
1 tbsp olive oil
2 tbsp butter, plus extra for greasing
salt
tomato and basil salad, to serve

SAUCE

¼ cup butter
1 onion, chopped
15 oz button mushrooms, trimmed
1 green bell pepper, cored, deseeded, and
sliced into thin rings
⅔ cup milk
3 eggs, beaten lightly
2 tbsp heavy cream
1 tsp dried oregano
pinch of finely grated nutmeg
freshly ground black pepper
1 tbsp freshly grated Parmesan

1 Cook the pasta in a large pan of salted boiling water, adding the olive oil. When almost tender, drain in a colander. Return the pasta to the pan, add the butter, and shake the pan well.

2 Grease an 8 in. loose-bottomed flan pan. Press the pasta onto the base of the pan and round the sides to form a case.

3 Heat the butter in a skillet over medium heat and fry the onion until it is translucent. Remove with a perforated spoon and spread in the flan base.

4 Add the mushrooms and bell pepper rings to the skillet and turn them in the butter until glazed. Fry for 2 minutes on each side, then arrange in the flan base.

5 Beat together the milk, eggs, and cream, stir in the oregano, and season with nutmeg and pepper. Pour the mixture carefully over the vegetables and sprinkle on the cheese.

6 Bake the flan in a preheated oven, 350°F, for 40–45 minutes, until the filling is set. Slide onto a serving plate and serve warm.

Step *3*

Step *4*

Step *5*

FISH DISHES

Italians eat everything that comes out of the sea, from the smallest whitebait to the massive tuna fish. Fish markets in Italy are fascinating, with a huge variety of fish on display, but as most of the fish comes from the Mediterranean it is not always easy to find an equivalent elsewhere. However, fresh or frozen imported fish of all kinds is increasingly appearing in fish stores and supermarkets.

After pasta, fish is probably the most important source of food in Italy, and in many recipes fish or seafood are combined with one type of pasta or another.

The inland regions of Italy, such as Lombardy and Umbria, have lakes with plentiful supplies of fish, while Apulia has abundant supplies caught by offshore trawlers. The south has splendid fish with tuna and swordfish taking pride of place, although red mullet and sea bass are plentiful and popular too. Venice and surrounding areas have a wealth of fish and seafood recipes, often combined with pasta. The Ligurian coast is well-known for its fish soups and stews. The islands of Sicily and Sardinia abound with fish which feature widely in their cuisine, including the sardines which give Sardinia its name.

Squid Casserole

Squid is often served fried in Italy, but here it is casseroled with tomatoes and bell peppers to give a rich sauce.

SERVES 4

INGREDIENTS

2 lb whole squid, cleaned or 1½ lb
squid rings, defrosted if frozen
3 tbsp olive oil
1 large onion, sliced thinly
2 garlic cloves, crushed
1 red bell pepper, cored, deseeded, and sliced
1–2 fresh rosemary sprigs
⅔ cup dry white wine and 1 cup water, or
1½ cups water or fish stock
14 oz can chopped tomatoes
2 tbsp tomato paste
1 tsp paprika
salt and pepper
fresh rosemary or parsley sprigs, to garnish

1 Cut the squid pouch into ½ in. slices; cut the tentacles into lengths of about 2 inches. If using frozen squid rings, make sure they are fully defrosted and well drained.

2 Heat the oil in a flameproof casserole and fry the onion and garlic gently until soft. Add the squid, increase the heat, and continue to cook for about 10 minutes until sealed and beginning to color lightly. Add the red bell pepper, rosemary, and wine, if using, and water or stock and bring up to a boil. Cover and simmer gently for 45 minutes.

3 Discard the sprigs of rosemary (but don't take out any leaves that have come off). Add the tomatoes, tomato paste, seasonings, and paprika. Continue to simmer gently for 45–60 minutes, or cover the casserole tightly and cook in a preheated oven, 350°F, for 45–60 minutes until tender.

4 Give the sauce a good stir, adjust the seasoning, and serve with crusty bread.

Step *1*

Step *2*

Step *3*

Baked Sea Bass

*Sea bass is a delicious white-fleshed fish. If cooking two small fish, they
can be broiled; if cooking one large fish, bake it in the oven.*

SERVES 4

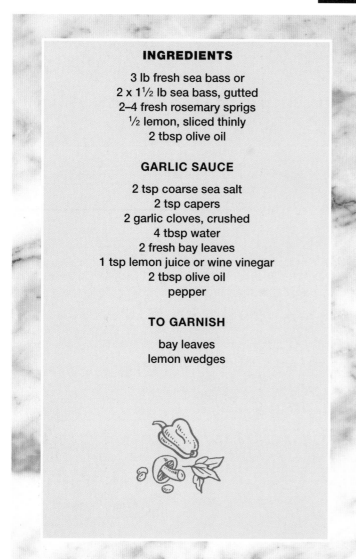

INGREDIENTS

3 lb fresh sea bass or
2 x 1½ lb sea bass, gutted
2–4 fresh rosemary sprigs
½ lemon, sliced thinly
2 tbsp olive oil

GARLIC SAUCE

2 tsp coarse sea salt
2 tsp capers
2 garlic cloves, crushed
4 tbsp water
2 fresh bay leaves
1 tsp lemon juice or wine vinegar
2 tbsp olive oil
pepper

TO GARNISH

bay leaves
lemon wedges

1 Scrape off the scales from the fish and cut off the sharp fins. Make diagonal cuts along both sides. Wash and dry thoroughly. Place a sprig of rosemary in the cavity of each of the smaller fish with half the lemon slices; or two sprigs and all the lemon in the large fish.

2 To broil, place in a foil-lined pan, brush lightly with 1–2 tablespoons oil, and broil under a moderate heat for about 5 minutes each side or until cooked through, turning carefully.

3 To bake: place the fish in a foil-lined dish or roasting pan brushed with oil, and brush the fish with the rest of the oil. Cook in a preheated oven, 375°F, for about 30 minutes for the small fish or 45–50 minutes for the large fish, until the thickest part of the fish is opaque.

4 For the sauce: crush the salt and capers with the garlic with a pestle and mortar if available and then gradually work in the water. Alternatively, put it all into a food processor or blender and process until smooth.

5 Bruise the bay leaves and remaining sprigs of rosemary and put in a bowl. Add the garlic mixture, lemon juice or vinegar, and oil and pound together until the flavors are released. Season with pepper.

6 Place the fish on a serving dish and, if liked, carefully remove the skin. Spoon some of the sauce over the fish and serve the rest separately. Garnish with fresh bay leaves and lemon wedges.

Step *1*

Step *4*

Step *5*

Trout in Red Wine

*This recipe from Trentino is best when the fish are freshly caught, but it is
a good way to cook any trout, giving it an interesting flavor.*

SERVES 4

INGREDIENTS

4 fresh trout, about 10 oz each
1 cup red or white wine vinegar
1¼ cups red or dry white wine
⅔ cup water
1 carrot, sliced
2–4 bay leaves
thinly pared rind of 1 lemon
1 small onion, sliced very thinly
4 fresh parsley sprigs
4 fresh thyme sprigs
1 tsp black peppercorns
6–8 whole cloves
6 tbsp butter
1 tbsp chopped fresh mixed herbs
salt and pepper

TO GARNISH

herb sprigs
lemon slices

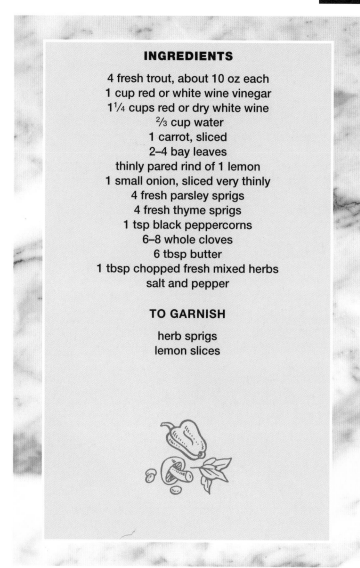

1 Gut the trout but leave their heads on. Dry on paper towels and lay the fish head to tail in a shallow container or roasting pan just large enough to hold them.

2 Bring the wine vinegar to a boil and pour slowly all over the fish. Leave the fish to marinate in the refrigerator for about 20 minutes.

3 Put the wine, water, carrot, bay leaves, lemon rind, onion, herbs, peppercorns, and cloves into a pan with a good pinch of sea salt and heat gently.

4 Drain the fish thoroughly, discarding the vinegar. Place the fish in a fish kettle or large skillet so they touch. When the wine mixture boils, strain gently over the fish so they are about half covered. Cover the kettle or skillet and simmer very gently for 15 minutes.

5 Carefully remove the fish from the kettle or skillet, draining off as much of the liquid as possible, and arrange on a serving dish. Keep warm.

6 Boil the cooking liquid hard until reduced to about 4–6 tablespoons. Melt the butter in a small saucepan and strain in the cooking liquor. Adjust the seasoning and spoon over the fish. Sprinkle with chopped mixed herbs and garnish with lemon and sprigs of herbs.

Step *1*

Step *3*

Step *4*

Sardine & Potato Bake

*Fresh sardines are now readily available, so this traditional dish from
Liguria can be enjoyed by all.*

SERVES 4

INGREDIENTS

2 lb potatoes
2 lb sardines, defrosted if frozen
1 tbsp olive oil, plus extra for oiling
1 onion, chopped
2–3 garlic cloves, crushed
2 tbsp chopped fresh parsley
12 oz ripe tomatoes, peeled and sliced
or 14 oz can peeled tomatoes, partly drained
and chopped
1–2 tbsp chopped fresh Italian herbs, such as
oregano, thyme, rosemary, marjoram
⅔ cup dry white wine
salt and pepper

1 Put the potatoes in a pan of salted water, bring to a boil, cover, and simmer for 10 minutes, then drain. When cool enough to handle, cut into slices about ¼ in. thick.

2 Gut and clean the sardines: cut off their heads and tails and then slit open the length of the belly. Turn the fish over so the skin is upward and press firmly along the backbone to loosen the bones. Turn over again and carefully remove the backbone. Wash the fish in cold water, drain well, and dry them on paper towels.

3 Heat the oil in a skillet and fry the onion and garlic until soft, but not colored.

4 Arrange the potatoes in a well-oiled ovenproof dish and sprinkle with the onions, then the parsley, and plenty of seasoning.

5 Lay the open sardines over the potatoes, skin-side down, then cover with the tomatoes and the rest of the herbs. Pour on the wine and season again.

6 Cook uncovered in a preheated oven, 180°F, for about 40 minutes until the fish is tender. If the casserole seems to be drying out, add another couple of tablespoons of wine.

Step *2*

Step *4*

Step *5*

Skewered Monkfish with Caper Sauce

Monkfish is a very meaty-textured fish. It cooks very well as it doesn't flake like most other fish.

SERVES 4

INGREDIENTS

1¹/₂ lb monkfish tail
finely grated rind and juice of 1 small lemon
2 tbsp olive oil
a small bunch of fresh bay leaves
1 small lemon, cut into wedges

SAUCE

6 tbsp olive oil
1 garlic clove, chopped finely
finely grated rind and juice of 1 small lemon
1 tbsp chopped fresh parsley
2 tbsp capers, drained and chopped
3 anchovy fillets, chopped finely
pepper

1 Wash and pat dry the monkfish using paper towels. Carefully trim away the pinky gray membrane, and slice either side the central bone to give 2 thick fillets.

2 Cut the monkfish into 1 in. cubes and place in a shallow dish. Toss in the lemon rind and juice and the olive oil.

3 Drain the fish, reserving the juices, and thread onto 4 bamboo skewers, threading a few bay leaves and wedges of lemon in between the fish cubes.

4 Preheat a broiler to medium. Place the skewers on a rack and cover the ends of the skewers with foil to prevent burning. Brush with some of the reserved juices and cook for 3 minutes. Turn over, brush again, and cook for a further 3–4 minutes until tender and cooked through.

5 Meanwhile, mix together all the ingredients for the sauce and set aside.

6 Drain the skewers and transfer to warm serving plates. Serve with the sauce and salad greens.

Step *1*

Step *3*

Step *5*

Pan-Fried Shrimp with Garlic

A luxurious dish which makes an impressive starter or light meal.

SERVES 4

INGREDIENTS

4 garlic cloves
20–24 unshelled large raw shrimp
8 tbsp butter
4 tbsp olive oil
6 tbsp brandy
salt and pepper
2 tbsp chopped fresh parsley

1 Peel and slice the garlic.

2 Wash the shrimp and pat dry using paper towels.

3 Melt the butter with the oil in a large skillet, add the garlic and shrimp, and fry over a high heat, stirring, for 3–4 minutes until the shrimp are pink.

4 Sprinkle with brandy and season to taste. Sprinkle with parsley and serve immediately with lemon wedges and Italian bread, if liked.

Step *1*

Step *3*

Step *4*

POULTRY &
MEAT DISHES

*Italians have their own special way of butchering meat,
producing very different cuts. Most meat is sold ready
boned and often cut straight across the grain.
Veal is a great favorite and widely available. Pork is
also popular, with roast pig being the traditional dish of
Umbria. Suckling pig is roasted with lots of fresh herbs,
especially rosemary, until the skin is crisp and brown.
Lamb is often served for special occasions, cooked
on a spit or roasted in the oven with wine, garlic, and
herbs; and the very small cutlets from young lambs
feature widely, especially in Rome. Variety meats play
an important role, with liver, brains, sweetbreads,
tongue, heart, tripe, and kidneys always available.
Poultry dishes provide some of Italy's finest food. Every
part of the chicken is used, including the feet and
innards for making soup. Spit-roasted chicken, flavored
strongly with rosemary, has become almost a national
dish. Turkey, capon, duck, goose, and guinea fowl are
also popular, as is game. Wild rabbit, hare, wild boar,
and deer are available, especially in Sardinia.*

Pan-Cooked Chicken with Artichokes

Artichokes are a familiar ingredient in Italian cookery.
In this dish, they are used to delicately flavor chicken.

SERVES 4

INGREDIENTS

4 chicken breasts, part boned
2 tbsp butter
2 tbsp olive oil
2 red onions, cut into wedges
2 tbsp lemon juice
⅔ cup dry white wine
⅔ cup chicken stock
2 tsp plain flour
14 oz can artichoke halves,
drained and halved
salt and pepper
chopped fresh parsley, to garnish

1 Season the chicken with salt and freshly ground black pepper. Heat the oil and 1 tablespoon of the butter in a large skillet. Add the chicken and fry for 4–5 minutes on each side until lightly golden. Remove from the skillet using a perforated spoon.

2 Toss the onion in the lemon juice, and add to the skillet. Gently fry, stirring, for 3–4 minutes until just beginning to soften.

3 Return the chicken to the skillet. Pour in the wine and stock, bring to a boil, cover, and simmer gently for 30 minutes.

4 Remove the chicken from the skillet, reserving the cooking juices, and keep warm. Bring the juices to a boil, and boil rapidly for 5 minutes.

5 Blend the remaining butter with the flour to form a paste. Reduce the juices to a simmer and drop the paste into the skillet, stirring until thickened.

6 Adjust the seasoning, stir in the artichoke hearts, and cook for a further 2 minutes. Pour over the chicken and garnish with parsley.

Step *1*

Step *3*

Step *5*

Barbecued Chicken

You need a bit of brute force to prepare the chicken, but once marinated,
it's an easy and tasty candidate for the barbecue.

SERVES 4

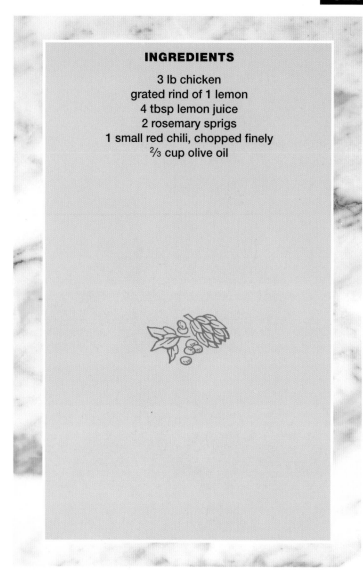

INGREDIENTS

3 lb chicken
grated rind of 1 lemon
4 tbsp lemon juice
2 rosemary sprigs
1 small red chili, chopped finely
⅔ cup olive oil

1 Split the chicken down the breast bone and open it out. Trim off excess fat, and remove the pope's nose, wing, and leg tips. Break the leg and wing joints to enable you to pound it flat. This ensures that it cooks evenly.

2 Cover the split chicken with plastic wrap and pound it as flat as possible with a rolling pin.

3 Mix the lemon rind and juice, rosemary sprigs, chili, and olive oil together in a small bowl. Place the chicken in a large dish and pour over the marinade, turning the chicken to coat it evenly. Cover the dish and leave the chicken to marinate for at least 2 hours.

4 Cook the chicken over a hot barbecue (the coals should be white, and red when fanned) for about 30 minutes, turning it regularly until the skin is golden and crisp. To test if it is cooked, pierce one of the chicken thighs; if it is ready, the juices should run clear, not pink. Serve with a salad.

Step *1*

Step *2*

Step *4*

Chicken with Green Olives

Olives are a popular flavoring for poultry and game in Apulia, where this recipe originates.

SERVES 4

INGREDIENTS

4 chicken breasts, part boned
2 tbsp butter
2 tbsp olive oil
1 large onion, chopped finely
2 garlic cloves, crushed
2 red, yellow, or green bell peppers, cored, deseeded, and cut into large pieces
8 oz large closed cup mushrooms, sliced or quartered
6 oz tomatoes, peeled and halved
⅔ cup dry white wine
4–6 oz green olives, pitted
4–6 tbsp heavy cream
salt and pepper
chopped flat-leaf parsley, to garnish

1 Season the chicken with salt and pepper. Heat the oil and butter in a skillet, add the chicken, and fry until browned all over. Remove from the skillet.

2 Add the onion and garlic to the skillet and fry gently until beginning to soften. Add the bell peppers to the skillet with the mushrooms and continue to cook for a few minutes longer.

3 Add the tomatoes and plenty of seasoning to the skillet, and then transfer the vegetable mixture to an ovenproof casserole. Place the chicken on the bed of vegetables.

4 Add the wine to the skillet and bring to a boil. Pour the wine over the chicken and cover the casserole tightly. Cook in a preheated oven, 350°F, for 50 minutes.

5 Add the olives to the chicken, mix lightly, then pour on the cream. Re-cover the casserole and return to the oven for 10–20 minutes or until the chicken is very tender.

6 Adjust the seasoning and serve the pieces of chicken, surrounded by the vegetables and sauce, with pasta or tiny new potatoes. Sprinkle with parsley to garnish.

Step *2*

Step *3*

Step *5*

Chicken Scallops

*Served in scallop shells, this makes a stylish presentation for a
dinner-party first course or a light lunch.*

SERVES 4

INGREDIENTS

6 oz short-cut macaroni, or other
short pasta shapes
3 tbsp vegetable oil, plus extra for brushing
1 onion, chopped finely
3 slices unsmoked lean bacon, rind
removed, chopped
4 oz button mushrooms, sliced thinly
or chopped
¾ cup diced cooked chicken
¾ cup crème fraîche
4 tbsp dry bread crumbs
½ cup grated sharp hard cheese
salt and pepper
flat-leaf parsley sprigs, to garnish

1 Cook the pasta in a large pan of boiling salted water
to which you have added 1 tablespoon of the oil.
When the pasta is almost tender, drain in a colander,
return to the pan, and cover.

2 Heat the broiler to medium. Heat the remaining oil
in a pan over medium heat and fry the onion until it
is translucent. Add the chopped bacon and mushrooms
and cook for a further 3–4 minutes, stirring.

3 Stir in the pasta, chicken, and crème fraîche and
season to taste with salt and pepper.

4 Brush 4 large scallop shells with oil. Spoon in the
chicken mixture and smooth to make neat mounds.

5 Mix together the bread crumbs and cheese, and
sprinkle over the top of the shells. Press the topping
lightly into the chicken mixture, and broil for 4–5
minutes, until golden brown and bubbling. Garnish with
parsley, and serve hot.

Step *2*

Step *3*

Step *5*

Roman Chicken

*This classic Roman dish makes an ideal light meal. It is equally good cold
and could be taken on a picnic – serve with bread to mop up the juices.*

SERVES 4

INGREDIENTS

4 tbsp olive oil
6 chicken pieces
2 garlic cloves, crushed with 1 tsp salt
1 large red onion, sliced
4 large mixed red, green, and yellow bell peppers,
cored, deseeded, and cut into strips
⅔ cup pitted green olives
½ quantity Tomato Sauce (page 44)
1¼ cups hot chicken stock
2 fresh marjoram sprigs
salt and pepper

1 Heat half the oil in a flameproof casserole and brown the chicken pieces on all sides. Remove the chicken pieces and set aside.

2 Add the remaining oil to the casserole and fry the garlic and onion until softened. Stir in the peppers, olives, and tomato sauce.

3 Return the chicken to the casserole with the stock and marjoram. Cover the casserole and simmer for about 45 minutes until the chicken is tender. Season to taste with salt and pepper, and serve with crusty bread.

Step *1*

Step *2*

Step *3*

Pizzaiola Steak

*This has a Neapolitan sauce, using the delicious red tomatoes so abundant
in that area, but canned ones make an excellent alternative.*

SERVES 4

INGREDIENTS

2 × 14 oz cans peeled tomatoes or
1½ lb fresh tomatoes
4 tbsp olive oil
2–3 garlic cloves, crushed
1 onion, chopped finely
1 tbsp tomato paste
1½ tsp chopped fresh marjoram or oregano
or ¾ tsp dried marjoram or oregano
4 thin sirloin or short loin steaks
2 tbsp chopped fresh parsley
1 tsp sugar
salt and pepper
fresh herbs, to garnish (optional)
sauté potatoes, to serve

1 If using canned tomatoes, purée them in a food processor, then strain to remove the seeds. If using fresh tomatoes, peel, remove the seeds, and chop finely.

2 Heat half the oil in a skillet and fry the garlic and onions very gently until soft – about 5 minutes.

3 Add the tomatoes, seasoning, tomato paste, and chopped herbs to the skillet. If using fresh tomatoes, add 4 tablespoons water too, and then simmer very gently for 8–10 minutes, giving an occasional stir.

4 Meanwhile, trim the steaks, if necessary, and season with salt and pepper. Heat the remaining oil in a skillet and fry the steaks quickly on both sides to seal, then continue until cooked to your liking – 2 minutes for rare, 3–4 minutes for medium, or 5 minutes for well done. Alternatively, cook the steaks under a hot broiler after brushing lightly with oil.

5 When the sauce has thickened a little, adjust the seasoning and stir in the chopped parsley and sugar.

6 Pour off the excess fat from the skillet with the steaks and add the tomato sauce. Reheat gently and serve at once, with the sauce spooned over and around the steaks. Garnish with fresh herbs, if liked. Sauté potatoes make a good accompaniment with a green vegetable.

Step *4*

Step *5*

Step *6*

Beef in Barolo

Barolo is a famous wine from the Piedmont area of Italy. Its mellow flavor is the key to this dish, so don't stint on the quality of the wine.

SERVES 6

INGREDIENTS

4 tbsp oil
2 lb piece boned rolled rib of beef,
or piece of round
2 garlic cloves, crushed
4 shallots, sliced
1 tsp chopped fresh rosemary
1 tsp chopped fresh oregano
2 celery stalks, sliced
1 large carrot, diced
2 cloves
1 bottle Barolo wine
freshly grated nutmeg
salt and pepper

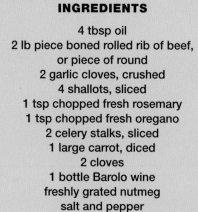

1 Heat the oil in a flameproof casserole and brown the meat all over. Remove the meat from the casserole.

2 Add the garlic, shallots, herbs, celery, carrot, and cloves to the casserole and fry for 5 minutes.

3 Replace the meat on top of the vegetables. Pour in the wine. Cover the casserole and simmer gently for about 2 hours until tender. Remove the meat from the casserole, slice, and keep warm.

4 Rub the contents of the pan through a strainer or purée in a blender, adding a little hot beef stock if necessary. Season to taste with nutmeg, salt, and pepper. Serve the meat with the sauce, accompanied by broccoli, carrots, and new potatoes.

Step *1*

Step *3*

Step *4*

Beef Olives in Rich Gravy

*Wafer-thin slices of tender beef with a rich garlic and
bacon stuffing, flavored with the tang of orange.*

SERVES 4

INGREDIENTS

8 ready prepared beef olives
4 tbsp chopped fresh parsley
4 garlic cloves, chopped finely
4 oz smoked fatty bacon, rinded
and chopped finely
grated rind of ½ small orange
2 tbsp olive oil
1¼ cups dry red wine
1 bay leaf
1 tsp sugar
2 oz pitted black olives, drained
salt and pepper

TO GARNISH

orange slices
chopped fresh parsley

1 Unroll the beef olives and flatten out as thinly as possible using a meat tenderizer or mallet. Trim the edges to neaten.

2 Mix together the parsley, garlic, bacon, orange rind, and seasoning. Spread this mixture evenly over each beef olive.

3 Roll up each olive tightly, then secure with a toothpick. Heat the oil in a skillet and fry the beef on all sides for 10 minutes.

4 Drain the beef olives, reserving the cooking juices, and keep warm. Pour the wine into the juices, add the bay leaf, sugar, and seasoning. Bring to a boil and boil rapidly for 5 minutes to reduce slightly.

5 Return the cooked beef to the skillet along with the olives and heat through for a further 2 minutes. Discard the bay leaf and toothpicks.

6 Transfer the beef olives and gravy to a serving dish, and serve garnished with orange slices and parsley.

Step *1*

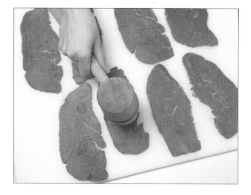

Step *3*

Step *4*

Saltimbocca

*Literally translated saltimbocca means "jump in the mouth",
and this quick, tasty veal dish almost does that.*

SERVES 4

INGREDIENTS

4 thin veal escalopes
8 fresh sage leaves
4 thin slices prosciutto (same size as the veal)
flour, for dredging
2 tbsp olive oil
2 tbsp butter
4 tbsp white wine
4 tbsp chicken stock
4 tbsp Marsala
salt and pepper
fresh sage leaves, to garnish

1 Either leave the escalopes as they are or cut them in half. Place the pieces of veal on a sheet of plastic wrap or baking parchment, keeping well apart, and cover with another piece.

2 Using a meat mallet or rolling pin, beat the escalopes gently until at least double in size and very thin.

3 Lightly season the escalopes with salt and pepper and lay two fresh sage leaves on the large slices, or one on each of the smaller slices. Then lay the prosciutto slices evenly over the escalopes to cover the sage and fit the size of the veal almost exactly.

4 Secure the prosciutto to the veal with wooden toothpicks. If preferred, the large slices can be folded in half first. Dredge lightly with a little flour.

5 Heat the olive oil and butter in a large skillet and fry the escalopes until golden brown on each side and just cooked through – about 4 minutes for single slices or 5–6 minutes for double ones. Take care not to overcook. Remove to a serving dish and keep warm.

6 Add the wine, stock, and Marsala to the skillet and bring to a boil, stirring well to loosen all the sediment from the base. Boil until reduced by almost half. Adjust the seasoning and quickly pour over the saltimbocca. Serve at once, garnished with fresh sage leaves.

Step *2*

Step *3*

Step *5*

Vitello Tonnato

Veal dishes are the specialty of Lombardy, with this dish being one of the more sophisticated. Serve cold with seasonal salads.

SERVES 4

INGREDIENTS

1½ lb boned leg of veal, rolled
2 bay leaves
10 black peppercorns
2–3 cloves
½ tsp salt
2 carrots, sliced
1 onion, sliced
2 celery stalks, sliced
3 cups stock or water
⅔ cup dry white wine (optional)
3 oz canned tuna fish, well drained
1½ oz can anchovy fillets, drained
⅔ cup olive oil
2 tsp bottled capers, drained
2 egg yolks
1 tbsp lemon juice
salt and pepper

TO GARNISH

capers
lemon wedges
fresh herbs

1 Put the veal in a saucepan with the bay leaves, peppercorns, cloves, salt, and vegetables. Add sufficient stock or water and the wine, if using, to barely cover the veal. Bring to a boil, remove any scum from the surface, then cover the pan, and simmer gently for an hour or so until tender. Leave in the water until cold, then drain thoroughly. If time allows, chill the veal to make it easier to carve.

2 For the tuna sauce: thoroughly mash the tuna with 4 anchovy fillets, 1 tablespoon oil, and the capers. Add the egg yolks and press through a strainer or purée in a food processor or liquidizer until smooth.

3 Stir in the lemon juice, then gradually beat in the rest of the oil, a few drops at a time, until the sauce is smooth and has the consistency of thick cream. Season with salt and pepper to taste.

4 Slice the veal thinly and arrange on a platter in overlapping slices. Spoon the sauce over the veal to cover. Then cover the dish and chill overnight.

5 Before serving, uncover the veal carefully. Arrange the remaining anchovy fillets and the capers in a decorative pattern on top, and garnish with lemon wedges and herbs.

Step *1*

Step *3*

Step *4*

Liver with Wine Sauce

Liver is popular in Italy and is served in many ways. Tender calf's liver is the best to use for this recipe, but you could use lamb's liver.

SERVES 4

INGREDIENTS

4 slices calf's liver or 8 slices lamb's liver, about 1 lb
flour, for coating
1 tbsp olive oil
2 tbsp butter
1 garlic clove, crushed
4 oz lean bacon slices, rinded and cut into narrow strips
1 onion, chopped
1 celery stalk, sliced thinly
⅔ cup red wine
⅔ cup beef stock
good pinch of ground allspice
1 tsp Worcestershire sauce
1 tsp chopped fresh sage or
½ tsp dried sage
3–4 tomatoes, peeled, quartered, and deseeded
salt and pepper
fresh sage leaves, to garnish
new potatoes or sauté potatoes, to serve

1 Wipe the liver, season with salt and pepper, and coat lightly in flour, shaking off the surplus.

2 Heat the oil and butter in a skillet and fry the liver until well sealed on both sides and just cooked through – take care not to overcook. Remove the liver from the skillet, cover, and keep warm, but do not allow to dry out.

3 Add the bacon to the fat left in the skillet, with the onion and celery. Fry gently until soft.

4 Add the wine, stock, allspice, Worcestershire sauce, and seasonings. Bring to a boil and simmer for 3–4 minutes.

5 Cut each tomato segment in half. Add to the sauce and continue to cook for a couple of minutes.

6 Serve the liver on a little of the sauce, with the remainder spooned over. Garnish with fresh sage leaves and serve with tiny new potatoes or sauté potatoes.

Step *1*

Step *2*

Step *4*

Pot Roasted Leg of Lamb

This dish from the Abruzzi uses a slow cooking method which ensures that the meat absorbs the flavorings and becomes very tender.

SERVES 4

INGREDIENTS

3½ lb leg of lamb
3–4 fresh rosemary sprigs
4 oz fatty bacon slices
4 tbsp olive oil
2–3 garlic cloves, crushed
2 onions, sliced
2 carrots, sliced
2 celery stalks, sliced
1¼ cups dry white wine
1 tbsp tomato paste
1¼ cups stock
12 oz tomatoes, peeled, quartered,
and deseeded
1 tbsp chopped fresh parsley
1 tbsp chopped fresh oregano or marjoram
salt and pepper
fresh rosemary sprigs, to garnish

1 Wipe the joint of lamb all over, trimming off any excess fat, then season well with salt and pepper, rubbing well in. Lay the sprigs of rosemary over the lamb, cover evenly with the bacon slices, and tie in place with fine string.

2 Heat the oil in a skillet and fry the lamb until browned all over, turning several times – about 10 minutes. Remove from the skillet.

3 Transfer the oil from the skillet to a large flameproof casserole and fry the garlic and onion together for 3–4 minutes until beginning to soften. Add the carrots and celery, and continue to cook for a few minutes longer.

4 Lay the lamb on top of the vegetables and press well to partly submerge. Pour the wine over the lamb, add the tomato paste, and simmer for 3–4 minutes. Add the stock, tomatoes, herbs, and seasoning and bring back to a boil for a further 3–4 minutes.

5 Cover the casserole tightly and cook in a preheated oven, 350°F, for 2–2½ hours until very tender.

6 Remove the lamb from the casserole and if liked, take off the bacon and herbs along with the string. Keep warm. Strain the juices, skimming off any excess fat, and serve in a pitcher. The vegetables may be put around the joint or in a serving dish. Garnish with fresh sprigs of rosemary.

Step *1*

Step *4*

Step *6*

Lamb with Olives

This is a very simple dish, and the chili gives it a kick. It is quick to prepare and makes an ideal supper dish.

SERVES 4

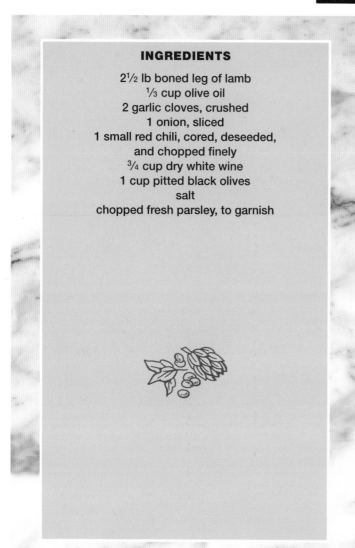

INGREDIENTS

2½ lb boned leg of lamb
⅓ cup olive oil
2 garlic cloves, crushed
1 onion, sliced
1 small red chili, cored, deseeded,
and chopped finely
¾ cup dry white wine
1 cup pitted black olives
salt
chopped fresh parsley, to garnish

1 Cut the lamb into 1 in. cubes.

2 Heat the oil in a skillet and fry the garlic, onion, and chili for 5 minutes.

3 Add the wine and meat and cook for a further 5 minutes.

4 Stir in the olives, then transfer the mixture to a casserole. Place in a preheated oven, 350°F, and cook for about 1 hour 20 minutes until the meat is tender. Season to taste with salt, and serve garnished with chopped fresh parsley.

Step *1*

Step *3*

Step *4*

Pork Chops with Sage

*The fresh taste of sage is the perfect ingredient
to counteract the richness of pork.*

SERVES 4

INGREDIENTS

2 tbsp flour
1 tbsp chopped fresh sage or 1 tsp dried sage
4 lean boneless pork chops, trimmed of excess fat
2 tbsp olive oil
1 tbsp butter
2 red onions, sliced into rings
1 tbsp lemon juice
2 tsp superfine sugar
4 plum tomatoes, quartered
salt and pepper

1 Mix the flour, sage, salt, and pepper on a plate. Lightly dust the pork chops on both sides with the seasoned flour.

2 Heat the oil and butter in a skillet, add the chops, and cook them for 6–7 minutes on each side until cooked through.

3 Drain the chops, reserving the cooking juices, and keep warm.

4 Toss the onion in the lemon juice and fry along with the sugar and tomatoes for 5 minutes until tender.

5 Serve the pork accompanied by the tomato and onion mixture and a green salad.

Step *1*

Step *2*

Step *4*

Pork Tenderloin Stuffed with Prosciutto

*A sophisticated roast with Mediterranean flavors
is ideal served with a pungent olive paste.*

SERVES 4

INGREDIENTS

1 lb piece of lean pork tenderloin
small bunch of fresh basil leaves, washed
2 tbsp freshly grated Parmesan
2 tbsp sun-dried tomato paste
6 thin slices prosciutto
1 tbsp olive oil
salt and pepper

OLIVE PASTE

⅔ cup pitted black olives
4 tbsp olive oil
2 garlic cloves, peeled

1 Trim away excess fat and membrane from the pork tenderloin. Slice the pork lengthwise down the middle, taking care not to cut all the way through.

2 Open out the pork and season the inside. Lay the basil leaves down the center. Mix the cheese and sun-dried tomato paste and spread on top of the basil.

3 Press the pork back together. Wrap the prosciutto around the pork, overlapping, to cover. Place on a rack in a roasting pan, seamside down, and brush with olive oil. Bake in a preheated oven, 375°F, for 30–40 minutes depending on thickness until cooked through. Allow to stand for 10 minutes.

4 For the olive paste, place all the ingredients in a blender or food processor and blend until smooth. Alternatively, for a coarser paste, finely chop the olives and garlic, and mix with the oil.

5 Drain the cooked pork and slice thinly to serve, accompanied with the olive paste and a salad.

Step *1*

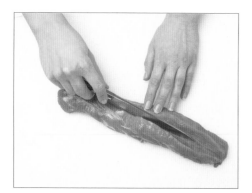

Step *3*

Step *4*

RICE, POLENTA, & GNOCCHI

Rice dishes are particularly popular in the north of Italy where a fair amount is consumed in risottos. Milanese and other risottos are made with short-grain Italian rice, the best of which is Arborio, but remember that this type of rice should be rinsed before using.
An Italian risotto is far moister than a pilau or other savory rice dish, but it should not be soggy or sticky. Gnocchi are made with maize flour, cornmeal (polenta), potatoes, or semolina, often combined with spinach or some sort of cheese. Gnocchi resemble dumplings and are either poached or baked, and served with a cheese sauce.
Polenta is made with either cornmeal or polenta flour and can be served either as a soft porridge or a firmer cake which is then fried until crisp. The traditional method of making polenta involved lengthy and laborious stirring, but there is now an excellent polenta mix available which cuts the time to 5 minutes!

Potato Gnocchi with Garlic & Herb Sauce

*These little potato dumplings are a traditional Italian appetizer but,
served with a salad and bread, they make a substantial meal.*

SERVES 4-6

INGREDIENTS

2 lb maincrop potatoes, cut into
½ in. pieces
¼ cup butter or margarine
1 egg, beaten
2½ cups all-purpose flour
salt

SAUCE

½ cup olive oil
2 garlic cloves, very finely chopped
1 tbsp chopped fresh oregano
1 tbsp chopped fresh basil
salt and pepper

TO SERVE

freshly grated Parmesan (optional)
mixed salad greens
warm Italian bread

1 Cook the potatoes in boiling salted water for about 10 minutes or until tender. Drain well.

2 Press the hot potatoes through a strainer into a large bowl. Add 1 teaspoon of salt, the butter or margarine, egg, and 1¼ cups of the flour. Mix well to bind together.

3 Turn onto a lightly floured surface and knead, gradually adding the remaining flour, until a smooth, soft, slightly sticky dough is formed.

4 Flour the hands and roll the dough into ¾ in. thick rolls. Cut into ½ in. pieces. Press the top of each one with the floured prongs of a fork and spread out on a floured dishcloth.

5 Bring a large saucepan of salted water to a simmer. Add the gnocchi and cook in batches for 2–3 minutes until they rise to the surface.

6 Remove with a perforated spoon and put in a warm, greased serving dish. Cover and keep warm.

7 To make the sauce, put the oil, garlic, and seasoning in a saucepan and cook gently, stirring, for 3–4 minutes until the garlic is golden. Remove from the heat and stir in the herbs. Pour over the gnocchi and serve immediately, sprinkled with Parmesan, if liked, and accompanied by salad and warm bread.

Step *2*

Step *3*

Step *4*

Gnocchi Romana

*This is a traditional recipe from Piedmont. For a less rich version, omit
the eggs. Serve as a starter, or a main meal with a crisp salad.*

SERVES 4

INGREDIENTS

3 cups milk
¼ tsp freshly grated nutmeg
6 tbsp butter, plus extra for greasing
1⅓ cups semolina
1 cup grated Parmesan
2 eggs, beaten
½ cup grated Swiss cheese
salt and pepper
basil sprigs, to garnish

1 Bring the milk to a boil, remove from the heat, and
stir in the seasoning, nutmeg, and 2 tablespoons of
butter. Gradually add the semolina, beating to prevent
lumps forming, and return to a low heat. Simmer gently
for about 10 minutes, stirring constantly, until very thick.

2 Beat ½ cup of Parmesan into the semolina, followed
by the eggs. Continue beating until the mixture is
quite smooth.

3 Spread out the semolina mixture in an even layer on a
sheet of baking parchment or on a large oiled cookie
sheet, smoothing the surface with a wet spatula – it
should be about ½ in. thick. Leave until cold, then chill
for about an hour until firm.

4 Cut the gnocchi into rounds about 1½ inches in
diameter, using a plain greased cookie cutter.

5 Thoroughly grease a shallow ovenproof dish, or
4 individual dishes. Lay the gnocchi trimmings in the
base of the dish and cover with overlapping circles of
gnocchi. Melt the remaining butter and drizzle all over
the gnocchi, then sprinkle first with the remaining
Parmesan, and then with the Swiss cheese.

6 Cook the gnocchi in a preheated oven, 400°F, for
25–30 minutes until the top is crisp and golden.

Step *2*

Step *3*

Step *4*

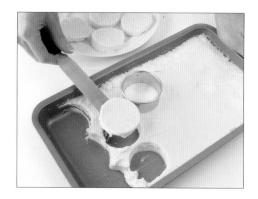

Spinach and Ricotta Gnocchi

Try not to handle the mixture too much when making gnocchi,
as this will make the dough a little heavy.

SERVES 4

INGREDIENTS

2 lb spinach
1½ cups Ricotta
1 cup grated Pecorino
3 eggs, beaten
¼ tsp freshly grated nutmeg
all-purpose flour
½ cup unsalted butter
¼ cup pine nuts
⅓ cup raisins
salt and pepper

1 Wash and drain the spinach well, and cook in a covered saucepan without any extra liquid until softened, about 8 minutes. Place in a colander and press well to remove as much juice as possible. Either rub through a strainer or purée in a blender.

2 Combine the spinach purée with the Ricotta, half the Pecorino, the eggs, nutmeg, and seasoning to taste, mixing lightly but thoroughly. Work in enough flour, lightly and quickly, to make the mixture easy to handle.

3 Shape the dough quickly into small lozenge shapes, and dust lightly with flour.

4 Add a dash of oil to a large pan of salted water and bring to a boil. Add the gnocchi carefully and boil for about 2 minutes until they float on the top. Use a perforated spoon and transfer to a buttered ovenproof dish. Keep warm.

5 Melt the butter in a skillet. Add the pine nuts and raisins and fry until the nuts start to brown slightly, but do not allow the butter to burn. Pour the mixture over the gnocchi and serve sprinkled with the remaining Pecorino.

Step *2*

Step *3*

Step *5*

Polenta

*Polenta is prepared and served in a variety of ways and can be served
hot or cold, sweet or savory.*

SERVES 4

INGREDIENTS

7 cups water
1½ tsp salt
2 cups polenta or cornmeal flour
2 beaten eggs (optional)
2 cups fresh fine white
bread crumbs (optional)
vegetable oil, for frying and oiling
2 quantities Basic Tomato Sauce (page 13)

MUSHROOM SAUCE

3 tbsp olive oil
8 oz mushrooms, sliced
2 garlic cloves, crushed
⅔ cup dry white wine
4 tbsp heavy cream
2 tbsp chopped fresh mixed herbs
salt and pepper

1 Bring the water and salt to a boil in a large pan and gradually sprinkle in the polenta or cornmeal flour, stirring all the time to prevent lumps forming.

2 Simmer the mixture very gently, stirring frequently, until the polenta becomes very thick and starts to draw away from the sides of the pan, about 30–35 minutes. It is likely to splatter, in which case partially cover the pan with a lid.

3 Thoroughly oil a shallow pan, about 11 × 7 inches, and spoon in the polenta. Spread out evenly, using a wet spatula. Allow to cool, then leave to stand for a few hours at room temperature, if possible.

4 Cut the polenta into 30–36 squares. Heat the oil in a skillet and fry the pieces until golden brown all over, turning several times – about 5 minutes. Alternatively, dip each piece of polenta in beaten egg, and coat in bread crumbs before frying in the hot oil.

5 To make the mushroom sauce: heat the oil in a pan and fry the mushrooms with the crushed garlic for 3–4 minutes. Add the wine, season well, and simmer for 5 minutes. Add the cream and chopped herbs and simmer for another minute or so.

6 Serve the polenta with either the tomato sauce or mushroom sauce.

Step *2*

Step *3*

Step *4*

Lazy Polenta with Rabbit Stew

*Polenta can be served fresh, as in this dish, or it can be cooled,
then sliced, and broiled.*

SERVES 4

INGREDIENTS

2 cups polenta or cornmeal
1 tbsp coarse sea salt
5 cups water
4 tbsp olive oil
4 lb rabbit pieces
3 garlic cloves, peeled
3 shallots, sliced
2/3 cup red wine
1 carrot, sliced
1 celery stalk, sliced
2 bay leaves
1 rosemary sprig
3 tomatoes, peeled and diced
1/2 cup pitted black olives
salt and pepper

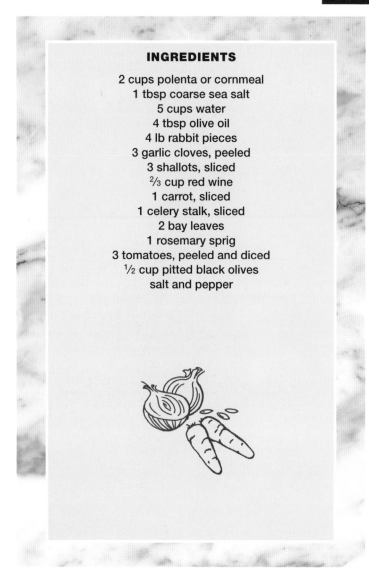

1 Butter a large ovenproof dish. Mix the polenta, salt, and water in a large saucepan, beating well to prevent lumps forming. Bring to a boil and boil for 10 minutes, stirring vigorously. Turn into the buttered dish and bake in a preheated oven, 375°F, for 40 minutes.

2 Meanwhile, heat the oil in a large saucepan and add the rabbit pieces, garlic, and shallots. Fry for 10 minutes until browned.

3 Stir in the wine and cook for a further 5 minutes.

4 Add the carrot, celery, bay leaves, rosemary, tomatoes, olives, and 1¼ cups water. Cover the pan and simmer for about 45 minutes until the rabbit is tender. Season to taste.

5 To serve, spoon or cut a portion of polenta and place on each serving plate. Top with a ladleful of stew.

Step *2*

Step *3*

Step *4*

Milanese Risotto

Italian rice is a round, short-grained variety with a nutty flavor, which is essential for a good risotto.

SERVES 4

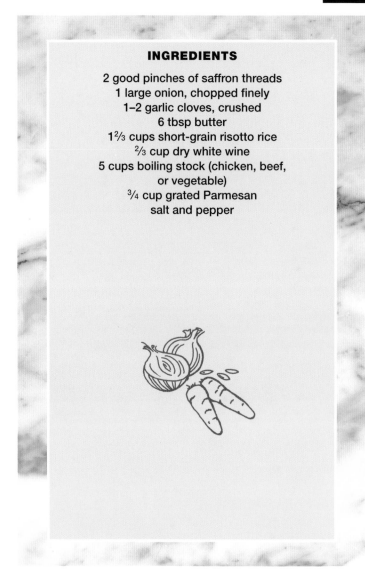

INGREDIENTS

2 good pinches of saffron threads
1 large onion, chopped finely
1–2 garlic cloves, crushed
6 tbsp butter
1²⁄₃ cups short-grain risotto rice
²⁄₃ cup dry white wine
5 cups boiling stock (chicken, beef, or vegetable)
¾ cup grated Parmesan
salt and pepper

1 Put the saffron in a small bowl, cover with 3–4 tablespoons boiling water, and leave to soak while cooking the risotto.

2 Fry the onion and garlic in 4 tablespoons of the butter until soft but not colored, then add the rice, and continue to cook for a few minutes until all the grains are coated in oil and beginning to color lightly.

3 Add the wine to the rice and simmer gently, stirring from time to time until it is all absorbed.

4 Add the boiling stock a little at a time, about ²⁄₃ cup, cooking until the liquid is fully absorbed before adding more, and stirring frequently.

5 When all the stock is absorbed the rice should be tender, but not soft and soggy. Add the saffron liquid, Parmesan, remaining butter, and plenty of seasoning. Simmer for a minute or so until piping hot and thoroughly mixed.

6 Cover the pan tightly and leave to stand for 5 minutes off the heat. Give a good stir and serve at once.

Step *1*

Step *2*

Step *5*

Rice and Peas

If you can get fresh peas (and willing helpers to shell them), do use them:
you will need 2 lb. Add to the pan with the stock.

SERVES 4

INGREDIENTS

1 tbsp olive oil
¼ cup butter
¼ cup Italian unsmoked bacon, chopped
1 small onion, chopped
6¼ cups hot chicken stock
1 cup risotto rice
3 tbsp chopped fresh parsley
1¼ cups frozen or
canned petits pois
½ cup grated Parmesan
pepper

1 Heat the oil with half the butter. Add the Italian unsmoked bacon and onion, and fry for 5 minutes. Add the stock and fresh peas, if using, and bring to a boil.

2 Stir in the rice and season to taste with pepper. Cook until the rice is tender, about 20–30 minutes, stirring occasionally.

3 Add the parsley and frozen or canned petits pois and cook for 8 minutes until the peas are thoroughly heated.

4 Stir in the remaining butter and the Parmesan. Serve immediately, with freshly ground black pepper.

Step *1*

Step *3*

Step *4*

PIZZAS

There is little to beat the irresistible aroma and taste of a freshly made pizza cooked in a wood-fired brick oven. However, a homemade dough base and a freshly made tomato sauce will give you the closest thing possible to an authentic Italian pizza.

Pizzas can have every imaginable type of topping. There are endless varieties of salamis and cured meats, hams and sausages, which all make excellent toppings. Canned or fresh fish or seafood are also good. The most popular fish for pizzas are anchovies and you either love them or hate them. If you find them too salty, soak them in a little milk before using.

Vegetables of all kinds make the most attractive and tempting pizza toppings. Choose the best quality vegetables and herbs for maximum flavor. A variety of antipasti are sold in jars of olive oil, such as artichoke hearts, sun-dried tomatoes, sliced bell peppers, and mushrooms. These make the most delicious and convenient toppings, and you can use the oil from the jar to drizzle over the pizza before baking to keep it moist.

Bread Dough Base

Traditionally, pizza bases are made from bread dough; this recipe will give you a base similar to an Italian pizza.

MAKES ONE 10 IN. PIZZA

INGREDIENTS

½ oz fresh yeast or 1 tsp dried
or easy-blend yeast
6 tbsp tepid water
½ tsp sugar
1 tbsp olive oil
6 oz all-purpose flour
1 tsp salt

1 Combine the fresh yeast with the water and sugar in a bowl. If using dried yeast, sprinkle it over the surface of the water and beat in until dissolved.

2 Leave the mixture to rest in a warm place for 10–15 minutes until frothy on the surface. Stir in the olive oil.

3 Sift the flour and salt into a large bowl. If using easy-blend yeast, stir it in at this point. Make a well in the center and pour in the yeast liquid, or water and oil (without the sugar for easy-blend yeast).

4 Using either floured hands or a wooden spoon, mix together to form a dough. Turn out onto a floured counter and knead for about 5 minutes until smooth and elastic.

5 Place in a large greased plastic bag and leave in a warm place for about 1 hour or until doubled in size.

6 Turn out onto a lightly floured counter and punch down the dough. This releases any air bubbles which would make the pizza uneven. Knead 4 or 5 times. The dough is now ready to use.

Step *3*

Step *4*

Step *6*

Biscuit Base

*This is a quick and easy alternative to the bread dough base. If you do not
have time to wait for bread dough to rise, a biscuit base is ideal.*

MAKES ONE 10 IN. BASE

INGREDIENTS

1½ cups self-rising flour
½ tsp salt
2 tbsp butter
½ cup milk

1 Sift the flour and salt into a bowl.

2 Rub in the butter with your fingertips until it resembles fine bread crumbs.

3 Make a well in the center of the flour and butter mixture and pour in nearly all the milk at once. Mix in quickly with a knife. Add the remaining milk only if necessary to mix to a soft dough.

4 Turn the dough out onto a floured counter and knead by turning and pressing with the heel of your hand 3 or 4 times.

5 Either roll out or press the dough into a 10 in. round on a lightly greased cookie sheet or pizza pan. Push up the edge slightly all round to form a ridge and use immediately.

Step 2

Step 4

Step 5

Potato Base

This is an unusual pizza base made from mashed potatoes and flour and is a great way to use up any leftover boiled potatoes.

MAKES ONE 10 IN. BASE

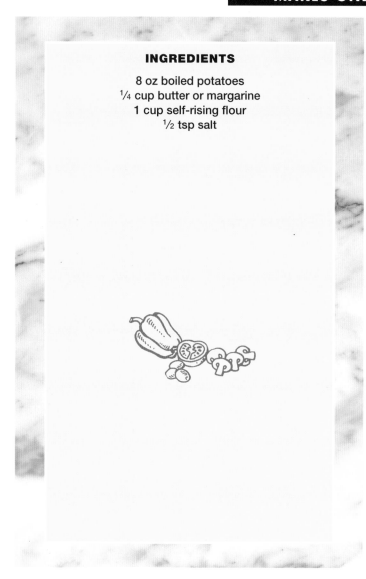

INGREDIENTS

8 oz boiled potatoes
¼ cup butter or margarine
1 cup self-rising flour
½ tsp salt

1 If the potatoes are hot, mash them, then stir in the butter until it has melted and is distributed evenly throughout the potatoes. Leave to cool.

2 Sift the flour and salt together and stir into the mashed potato to form a soft dough.

3 If the potatoes are cold, mash them without adding the butter. Sift the flour and salt into a bowl. Rub in the butter with your fingertips until the mixture resembles fine bread crumbs, then stir the flour and butter mixture into the mashed potatoes to form a soft dough.

4 Either roll out or press the dough into a 10 in. round on a lightly greased cookie sheet or pizza pan, pushing up the edge slightly all round to form a ridge before adding the topping. This base is tricky to lift before it is cooked, so you will find it easier to handle if you roll it out directly onto the cookie sheet.

5 If the base is not required for cooking immediately, you can cover it with plastic wrap and chill it for up to 2 hours.

Step *2*

Step *3*

Step *4*

Tomato Sauce

Using canned chopped tomatoes for this dish saves time, and they are preferable to plum tomatoes which tend to be watery.

MAKES ¾ CUP

INGREDIENTS

1 small onion, chopped
1 garlic clove, crushed
1 tbsp olive oil
7 oz can chopped tomatoes
2 tsp tomato paste
½ tsp sugar
½ tsp dried oregano
1 bay leaf
salt and pepper

1 Fry the onion and garlic gently in the oil for 5 minutes until softened but not browned.

2 Add the tomatoes, tomato paste, sugar, oregano, bay leaf, and seasoning. Stir well.

3 Bring to a boil, cover, and simmer gently for 20 minutes, stirring occasionally, until you have a thickish sauce.

4 Remove the bay leaf and adjust the seasoning to taste. Leave to cool completely before using. This sauce keeps well in a screw-top jar in the refrigerator for up to 1 week.

Step *1*

Step *2*

Step *4*

Special Tomato Sauce

This sauce is made with fresh tomatoes. Use the plum variety whenever available and always choose the reddest ones for the best flavor.

MAKES ¾ CUP

INGREDIENTS

1 small onion, chopped
1 small red bell pepper, chopped
1 garlic clove, crushed
2 tbsp olive oil
8 oz tomatoes
1 tbsp tomato paste
1 tsp soft brown sugar
2 tsp chopped fresh basil
½ tsp dried oregano
1 bay leaf
salt and pepper

1 Fry the onion, bell pepper, and garlic gently in the oil for 5 minutes until softened but not browned.

2 Cut a cross in the base of each tomato and place them in a bowl. Pour on boiling water and leave for about 45 seconds. Drain, and then plunge in cold water. The skins will slide off easily.

3 Chop the tomatoes, discarding any hard cores. Add to the onion mix with the tomato paste, sugar, herbs, and seasoning. Stir well. Bring to a boil, cover, and simmer gently for 30 minutes, stirring occasionally, until you have a thickish sauce.

4 Remove the bay leaf and adjust the seasoning to taste. Leave to cool completely before using.

5 This sauce will keep well in a screw-top jar in the refrigerator for up to 1 week.

Step *1*

Step *2*

Step *3*

Four Seasons

*This is a traditional pizza on which the toppings are divided into
4 sections, each of which is supposed to depict a season of the year.*

SERVES 2–4

INGREDIENTS

Bread Dough Base (page 186)
Special Tomato Sauce (page 194)
1 oz chorizo sausage, sliced thinly
1 oz button mushrooms, wiped
and sliced thinly
1½ oz artichoke hearts, sliced thinly
1 oz Mozzarella, sliced thinly
3 anchovies, halved lengthwise
2 tsp capers
4 pitted black olives, sliced
4 fresh basil leaves, shredded
olive oil for drizzling
salt and pepper

1 Roll out or press the dough, using a rolling pin or
your hands, into a 10 in. round on a lightly floured
counter. Place on a large greased cookie sheet or pizza
pan and push up the edge a little.

2 Cover and leave to rise slightly for 10 minutes in a
warm place before spreading with tomato sauce
almost to the edge.

3 Put the sliced chorizo onto one fourth of the pizza,
the sliced mushrooms on another, the artichoke
hearts on a third, and the Mozzarella and anchovies on
the fourth.

4 Dot the with the capers, olives, and basil leaves.
Drizzle with a little olive oil and season. Do not put
any salt on the anchovy section as the fish are very salty.

5 Bake in a preheated oven, 400°F, for 18–20 minutes,
or until the crust is golden and crisp. Serve
immediately.

Step *1*

Step *3*

Step *4*

Calabrian Pizza

Traditionally, this pizza has a double layer of dough to make it robust and filling. Alternatively, it can be made as a single pizza (as shown here).

SERVES 4–6

INGREDIENTS

3½ cups all-purpose flour
½ tsp salt
1 packet easy-blend yeast
2 tbsp olive oil
generous 1 cup warm water

FILLING

2 tbsp olive oil
2 garlic cloves, crushed
1 red bell pepper, cored, deseeded, and sliced
1 yellow bell pepper, cored, deseeded, and sliced
4 oz Ricotta
6 oz jar sun-dried tomatoes, drained
3 hard-cooked eggs, sliced thinly
1 tbsp chopped fresh mixed herbs
4 oz salami, cut into strips
5–6 oz Mozzarella, grated
a little milk, to glaze
salt and pepper

1 Sift the flour and salt into a bowl and mix in the easy-blend yeast. Add the olive oil and enough warm water to mix to a smooth pliable dough. Knead for 10–15 minutes by hand, or process for 5 minutes in a mixer.

2 Shape the dough into a ball, place in a lightly oiled plastic bag, and put in a warm place for 1–1½ hours or until doubled in size.

3 For the filling: heat the oil in a skillet and fry the garlic and bell peppers slowly in the oil until soft.

4 Punch down the dough and roll out half to fit the base of a 12 × 10 in. oiled roasting pan.

5 Season the dough and spread with the Ricotta, then cover with sun-dried tomatoes, hard-cooked eggs, herbs, and the pepper mixture. Arrange the salami strips on top and sprinkle with the grated cheese.

6 Roll out the remaining dough and place over the filling, sealing the edges well, or use to make a second pizza. Leave to rise for 1 hour in a warm place. An uncovered pizza will take only about 30–40 minutes to rise.

7 Prick the double pizza with a fork about 20 times, brush the top with milk, and cook in a preheated oven, 350°F, for about 50 minutes or until lightly browned. The uncovered pizza will take only 35–40 minutes. Serve hot.

Step *1*

Step *4*

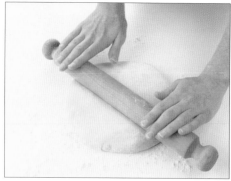

Step *5*

Smoky Bacon & Pepperoni

This more traditional kind of pizza is topped with pepperoni, smoked bacon, and bell peppers covered in a smoked cheese.

SERVES 2–4

INGREDIENTS

Bread Dough Base (page 186)
1 tbsp olive oil
1 tbsp freshly grated Parmesan
Tomato Sauce (page 192)
4 oz lightly smoked bacon, diced
½ green bell pepper, sliced thinly
½ yellow bell pepper, sliced thinly
2 oz pepperoni-style sliced spicy sausage
2 oz smoked Bavarian cheese, grated
½ tsp dried oregano
olive oil for drizzling
salt and pepper

1 Roll out or press the dough, using a rolling pin or your hands, into a 10 in. round on a lightly floured counter. Place on a large greased cookie sheet or pizza pan and push up the edge a little with your fingers, to form a rim.

2 Brush the base with the olive oil and sprinkle with the Parmesan. Cover and leave to rise slightly in a warm place for about 10 minutes.

3 Spread the tomato sauce over the base almost to the edge. Top with the bacon and bell peppers. Arrange the pepperoni on top and sprinkle generously with the smoked cheese.

4 Sprinkle over the oregano and drizzle with a little olive oil. Season well.

5 Bake in a preheated oven, 400°F, for 18–20 minutes, or until the crust is golden and crisp around the edge. Cut into wedges and serve immediately.

Step *2*

Step *3*

Step *4*

Calzone

A calzone is like a pizza in reverse – it resembles a large pasty with the dough on the outside and the filling on the inside.

SERVES 2–4

INGREDIENTS

Bread Dough Base (page 186)
1 egg, beaten
1 tomato, peeled and chopped
1 tbsp tomato paste
1 oz Italian salami, chopped
1 oz mortadella, chopped
1 oz Ricotta
2 scallions, trimmed and chopped
¼ tsp dried oregano
salt and pepper

1 Roll out the dough into a 9 in. round on a lightly floured counter. Brush the edge of the dough with a little beaten egg.

2 Spread the tomato paste over half the round nearest to you. Scatter the salami, mortadella, and chopped tomato on top. Dot with the Ricotta and sprinkle over the scallions and oregano. Season well.

3 Fold over the other half of the dough to form a half moon. Press the edges together well to prevent the filling from coming out.

4 Place on a cookie sheet and brush with beaten egg to glaze. Make a hole in the top to allow steam to escape.

5 Bake in a preheated oven, 400°F, for 20 minutes, or until golden.

Step *1*

Step *2*

Step *3*

Avocado & Ham

*A smoked ham and avocado salad is served on a pizza with a base
enriched with chopped sun-dried tomatoes and black olives.*

SERVES 2-4

INGREDIENTS

Bread Dough Base (page 186)
4 sun-dried tomatoes, chopped
1 oz black olives, chopped
Special Tomato Sauce (page 194)
4 small endive leaves, shredded
4 small radicchio leaves, shredded
1 avocado, peeled, pitted, and sliced
2 oz wafer-thin smoked ham
2 oz blue cheese, cut into small pieces
olive oil for drizzling
salt and pepper
chopped fresh chervil, to garnish

1 Knead the dough gently with the sun-dried tomatoes and olives until well mixed.

2 Roll out or press the dough, using a rolling pin or your hands, into a 10 in. round on a lightly floured counter. Place on a greased cookie sheet or pizza pan and push up the edge a little to form a rim.

3 Cover and leave to rise slightly in a warm place for 10 minutes before spreading with tomato sauce almost to the edge.

4 Top the pizza with shredded lettuce leaves and avocado slices. Scrunch up the ham and add with the cheese. Drizzle with a little olive oil and season well.

5 Bake in a preheated oven, 400°F, for 18–20 minutes, or until the edge is crisp and golden brown.

6 Sprinkle with chervil to garnish and serve immediately.

Step *1*

Step *3*

Step *6*

Spicy Meatball

Small ground beef meatballs, spiced with chilies and cumin seeds, are baked on a biscuit base.

SERVES 2-4

INGREDIENTS

8 oz ground lean beef
1 oz jalapeño chilies in brine, chopped
1 tsp cumin seeds
1 tbsp chopped fresh parsley
1 tbsp beaten egg
3 tbsp olive oil
Biscuit Base (page 188)
Tomato Sauce (page 192)
1 oz canned pimiento, sliced
2 slices fatty bacon, cut into strips
2 oz grated sharp hard cheese
olive oil for drizzling
salt and pepper
chopped fresh parsley, to garnish

1 Mix the beef, chilies, cumin seeds, parsley, and egg together in a bowl and season. Form into 12 small meatballs. Cover and chill for 1 hour.

2 Heat the oil in a large skillet. Add the meatballs and brown all over. Remove with a perforated spoon or slice and drain on paper towels.

3 Roll out or press the dough into a 10 in. round on a lightly floured counter. Place on a greased cookie sheet or pizza pan and push up the edge slightly to form a rim. Spread with the tomato sauce almost to the edge.

4 Arrange the meatballs on the pizza with the pimiento and bacon. Sprinkle over the cheese and drizzle with a little olive oil. Season.

5 Bake in a preheated oven, 400°F, for 18–20 minutes, or until the edge is golden and crisp. Serve immediately, garnished with chopped parsley.

Step *2*

Step *3*

Step *4*

American Hot Chili Beef

*This deep-pan pizza is topped with ground beef, red kidney beans, and
jalapeño chilies, which are small, green, and very hot.*

SERVES 2–4

INGREDIENTS

FOR THE DOUGH BASE

¾ oz fresh yeast or 1½ tsp dried or
easy-blend yeast
½ cup tepid water
1 tsp sugar
3 tbsp olive oil
2 cups all-purpose flour
1 tsp salt

FOR THE TOPPING

1 small onion, sliced thinly
1 garlic clove, crushed
½ yellow bell pepper, chopped
1 tbsp olive oil
6 oz lean ground beef
¼ tsp chili powder
¼ tsp ground cumin
7 oz can red kidney beans, drained
Tomato Sauce (page 192)
1 oz jalapeño chilies, sliced
2 oz Mozzarella, sliced thinly
2 oz sharp Cheddar or
Monterey Jack, grated
olive oil for drizzling
salt and pepper
chopped parsley, to garnish

1 For the deep-pan dough base, use the same method as the Bread Dough Base recipe (page 186).

2 Roll out or press the dough, using a rolling pin or your hands, into a 9 in. round on a lightly floured counter. Place on a large greased cookie sheet or pizza pan and push up the edge to form a small ridge. Cover and leave to rise slightly for about 10 minutes.

3 Fry the onion, garlic, and bell pepper gently in the oil for 5 minutes until soft but not browned. Increase the heat slightly and add the beef, chili, and cumin. Fry for 5 minutes, stirring occasionally. Remove from the heat and stir in the kidney beans. Season well.

4 Spread the tomato sauce over the dough almost to the edge and top with the meat mixture.

5 Top with the sliced chilies and Mozzarella and sprinkle over the grated cheese. Drizzle with a little olive oil and season.

6 Bake in a preheated oven, 400°F, for 18–20 minutes, or until the crust is golden. Serve immediately sprinkled with chopped parsley.

Step *3*

Step *4*

Step *5*

Breakfast Pizza

Sausages, bacon, and mushrooms on a bread base topped with a fried egg
will probably see you through the day.

SERVES 4

INGREDIENTS

Bread Dough Base (page 186)
12 small skinless sausages
3 tbsp oil
Tomato Sauce (page 192)
5 oz can baked beans in tomato sauce
4 slices lean bacon
2 oz baby button mushrooms, wiped
and quartered
1 small tomato, cut into 8 wedges
2 oz sharp hard cheese, grated
4 eggs
salt and pepper

1 Roll out or press the dough, using a rolling pin or your hands, into a 10 in. round on a lightly floured counter. Place on a large greased cookie sheet or pizza pan and push up the edge slightly to form a rim. Cover and leave to rise slightly for 10 minutes in a warm place.

2 Brown the sausages in a skillet with 1 tablespoon of the oil.

3 Mix the tomato sauce with the baked beans and spread over the base almost to the edge. Arrange the sausages on top.

4 Cut the bacon into strips and arrange on the pizza with the mushrooms and tomato. Sprinkle over the cheese and season.

5 Bake in a preheated oven, 400°F, for 18–20 minutes, or until the edge is crisp and golden brown.

6 Add the remaining oil to the skillet and fry the eggs. When the pizza is cooked, cut into four and top each with a fried egg. Serve immediately.

Step *3*

Step *4*

Step *6*

Funny Faces

These individual pizzas have faces made from sliced vegetables and pasta.
Children love pizzas and will enjoy making their own funny faces.

SERVES 4

INGREDIENTS

Bread Dough Base (page 186)
1 oz spaghetti or egg noodles
Tomato Sauce (page 192)
8 slices pepperoni-style sausage
8 thin slices celery
4 slices button mushrooms
4 slices yellow bell pepper
4 slices Mozzarella
4 slices zucchini
olive oil for drizzling
8 cooked peas

1 Divide the dough into 4. Roll each piece out into a 5 in. diameter round and place on greased cookie sheets. Cover and leave to rise slightly in a warm place for about 10 minutes.

2 Cook the spaghetti or egg noodles according to the packet instructions.

3 Divide the tomato sauce evenly between each pizza base and spread out almost to the edge.

4 To make the faces, use pepperoni slices for the main part of the eyes, celery for the eyebrows, mushrooms for the noses, and bell pepper slices for the mouths.

5 Cut the Mozzarella and zucchini slices in half. Use the cheese for the cheeks and the zucchini for ears.

6 Drizzle a little olive oil over each pizza and bake in a preheated oven, 400°F, for 12–15 minutes until the edges are crisp and golden.

7 Transfer the pizzas to serving plates and place the peas in the center of the eyes. Drain the spaghetti or noodles and arrange around the tops of the pizzas for hair. Serve immediately.

Step *4*

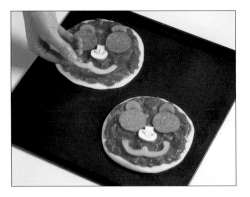

Step *6*

Step *7*

Eggplant & Lamb

An unusual fragrant, spiced pizza topped with ground lamb and eggplant on a bread base.

SERVES 2-4

INGREDIENTS

1 small eggplant, diced
Bread Dough Base (page 186)
1 small onion, sliced thinly
1 garlic clove, crushed
1 tsp cumin seeds
1 tbsp olive oil
6 oz ground lamb
1 oz canned pimiento, thinly sliced
2 tbsp chopped fresh cilantro
Special Tomato Sauce (page 194)
3 oz Mozzarella, sliced thinly
olive oil for drizzling
salt and pepper

1 Sprinkle the diced eggplant with salt in a colander and let the bitter juices drain for about 20 minutes; then rinse. Pat dry with paper towels.

2 Roll out or press the dough, using a rolling pin or your hands, into a 10 in. round on a lightly floured counter. Place on a large greased cookie sheet or pizza pan and push up the edge to form a rim.

3 Cover and leave to rise slightly for 10 minutes in a warm place.

4 Fry the onion, garlic, and cumin seeds gently in the oil for 3 minutes. Increase the heat slightly and add the lamb, eggplant, and pimiento. Fry for 5 minutes, stirring occasionally. Add the cilantro and season well.

5 Spread the tomato sauce over the dough base almost to the edge. Top with the lamb mixture.

6 Arrange the Mozzarella slices on top. Drizzle over a little olive oil and season.

7 Bake in a preheated oven, 400°F, for 18–20 minutes, until the crust is crisp and golden. Serve immediately.

Step *1*

Step *4*

Step *6*

Marinara

This pizza is topped with mixed seafood, such as shrimp, mussels, cockles, and squid rings.

SERVES 2–4

INGREDIENTS

Potato Base (page 190)
Special Tomato Sauce (page 194)
7 oz frozen seafood cocktail, defrosted
1 tbsp capers
1 small yellow bell pepper, cored, deseeded, and chopped
1 tbsp chopped fresh marjoram
½ tsp dried oregano
2 oz Mozzarella, grated
½ oz Parmesan, grated
12 black olives
olive oil for drizzling
salt and pepper
fresh marjoram or oregano sprig, to garnish

1 Roll out or press out the potato dough, using a rolling pin or your hands, into a 10 in. round on a lightly floured counter. Place on a large greased cookie sheet or pizza pan and push up the edge a little with your fingers to form a rim.

2 Spread the tomato sauce evenly over the base almost to the edge.

3 Arrange the seafood cocktail, capers, and yellow bell pepper on top of the sauce.

4 Sprinkle over the herbs and cheeses. Arrange the olives on top. Drizzle over a little olive oil and season generously with salt and pepper.

5 Bake in a preheated oven, 400°F, for 18–20 minutes until the edge of the pizza is crisp and golden brown.

6 Transfer to a warm serving plate, garnish with a sprig of marjoram or oregano, and serve immediately.

Step *2*

Step *3*

Step *4*

Florentine

A pizza adaptation of Eggs Florentine – sliced hard-cooked eggs on freshly cooked spinach, with a crunchy almond topping.

SERVES 2-4

INGREDIENTS

2 tbsp freshly grated Parmesan
Potato Base (page 190)
Tomato Sauce (page 192)
6 oz spinach
1 small red onion, sliced thinly
2 tbsp olive oil
¼ tsp freshly grated nutmeg
2 hard-cooked eggs
½ oz fresh white bread crumbs
2 oz Jarlsberg, grated (or Swiss cheese, if not available)
2 tbsp slivered almonds
olive oil for drizzling
salt and pepper

1 Mix the Parmesan with the potato base. Roll out or press the dough, using a rolling pin or your hands, into a 10 in. round on a lightly floured counter. Place on a large greased cookie sheet or pizza pan and push up the edge slightly. Spread the tomato sauce almost to the edge.

2 Remove the stalks from the spinach and wash the leaves thoroughly in plenty of cold water. Drain well and pat off the excess water with paper towels.

3 Fry the onion gently in the oil for 5 minutes until softened. Add the spinach and continue to fry until just wilted. Drain off any excess liquid. Place on the pizza and sprinkle over the nutmeg.

4 Remove the shells from the eggs and slice. Arrange on top of the spinach.

5 Mix together the bread crumbs, cheese, and almonds, and sprinkle over. Drizzle with a little olive oil and season well.

6 Bake in a preheated oven, 400°F, for 18–20 minutes, or until the edge is crisp and golden. Serve immediately.

Step *1*

Step *3*

Step *4*

Alaska Pizza

You can use either red or pink canned salmon to top this tasty pizza.
Red salmon has a better color and flavor, but it can be expensive.

SERVES 2–4

INGREDIENTS

Biscuit Base (page 188)
Tomato Sauce (page 192)
1 zucchini, grated
1 tomato, sliced thinly
3½ oz can red or pink salmon, drained
2 oz button mushrooms, wiped and sliced
1 tbsp chopped fresh dill
½ tsp dried oregano
1½ oz Mozzarella, grated
olive oil for drizzling
salt and pepper
fresh dill sprig, to garnish

1 Roll out or press the dough, using a rolling pin or your hands, into a 10 in. round on a lightly floured counter. Place on a large greased cookie sheet or pizza pan and push up the edge a little with your fingers to form a rim.

2 Spread the tomato sauce evenly over the pizza almost to the edge.

3 Sprinkle the tomato sauce with the grated zucchini, then lay the tomato slices on top.

4 Remove any bones and skin from the salmon and flake with a fork. Arrange on the pizza with the mushrooms. Sprinkle over the herbs and cheese. Drizzle with a little olive oil and season well.

5 Bake in a preheated oven, 400°F, for 18–20 minutes, or until the edge is golden and crisp. Transfer to a warm serving plate and serve immediately, garnished with a sprig of dill.

Step *3*

Step *4*

Step *5*

Herbed Onion with Anchovies

This tasty onion pizza is topped with a lattice pattern of anchovies and black olives. Cut the pizza into squares to serve.

MAKES 6 SQUARES

INGREDIENTS

4 tbsp olive oil
3 onions, sliced thinly
1 garlic clove, crushed
1 tsp soft brown sugar
½ tsp crushed fresh rosemary
7 oz can chopped tomatoes
Bread Dough Base (page 186)
2 tbsp freshly grated Parmesan
1¾ oz can anchovies
12–14 black olives
salt and pepper

1 Heat 3 tablespoons of the oil in a large saucepan and add the onions, garlic, sugar, and rosemary. Cover and fry gently for 10 minutes until the onions are soft but not brown, stirring occasionally. Add the tomatoes, stir, and season well. Leave to cool slightly.

2 Roll out or press the dough, using a rolling pin or your hands, on a lightly floured counter to fit a 12 × 7 in. greased jelly roll pan. Place in the pan and push up the edges slightly.

3 Brush the remaining oil over the dough and sprinkle with the cheese. Cover and leave to rise slightly in a warm place for about 10 minutes.

4 Spread the onion and tomato topping over the base. Drain the anchovies, reserving the oil. Split each anchovy in half lengthwise and arrange on the pizza in a lattice pattern. Place olives in between the anchovies and drizzle over a little of the reserved oil. Season.

5 Bake in a preheated oven, 400°F, for 18–20 minutes, or until the edges are crisp and golden. Cut into squares and serve immediately.

Step *1*

Step *2*

Step *4*

Roasted Vegetable & Goat's Cheese

Wonderfully colorful vegetables are roasted in olive oil with thyme and garlic. The goat's cheese adds a nutty, piquant flavor.

SERVES 2-4

INGREDIENTS

2 baby zucchini, halved lengthwise
2 baby eggplants, quartered lengthwise
½ red bell pepper, cut into 4 strips
½ yellow bell pepper, cut into 4 strips
1 small red onion, cut into wedges
2 garlic cloves, unpeeled
4 tbsp olive oil
1 tbsp red wine vinegar
1 tbsp chopped fresh thyme
Bread Dough Base (page 186)
Tomato Sauce (page 192)
3 oz goat's cheese
salt and pepper
fresh basil leaves, to garnish

1 Place all the prepared vegetables in a large roasting pan. Mix together the olive oil, vinegar, thyme, and plenty of seasoning and pour over, coating well.

2 Roast the vegetables in a preheated oven, 400°F, for 15–20 minutes until the skins have started to blacken in places, turning half-way through. Leave to rest for 5 minutes after roasting.

3 Carefully peel off the skins from the roast bell peppers and the garlic cloves. Slice the garlic.

4 Roll out or press the dough, using a rolling pin or your hands, into a 10 in. round on a lightly floured counter. Place on a large greased cookie sheet or pizza pan and raise the edge a little. Cover and leave for 10 minutes to rise slightly in a warm place. Spread with the tomato sauce almost to the edge.

5 Arrange the roasted vegetables on top and dot with the cheese. Drizzle the oil and juices from the roasting pan over the pizza and season.

6 Bake in a preheated oven, 400°F, for 18–20 minutes, or until the edge is crisp and golden. Serve immediately, garnished with basil leaves.

Step *1*

Step *3*

Step *5*

Mixed Bell Peppers & Red Onion

The vibrant colors of the bell peppers and onion make this a delightful pizza. Served cut into fingers, it is ideal for a party or buffet.

MAKES 8

INGREDIENTS

Bread Dough Base (page 186)
2 tbsp olive oil
½ each red, green, and yellow bell pepper, sliced thinly
1 small red onion, sliced thinly
1 garlic clove, crushed
Tomato Sauce (page 192)
3 tbsp raisins
1 oz pine nuts
1 tbsp chopped fresh thyme
olive oil for drizzling
salt and pepper

1 Roll out or press the dough, using a rolling pin or your hands, on a lightly floured counter to fit a 12 × 7 in. greased jelly roll pan. Place in the pan and push up the edges slightly.

2 Cover and leave to rise slightly in a warm place for about 10 minutes.

3 Heat the oil in a large skillet. Add the bell peppers, onion, and garlic, and fry gently for 5 minutes until they have softened but not browned. Leave to cool.

4 Spread the tomato sauce over the base of the pizza almost to the edge.

5 Sprinkle over the raisins and top with the cooled bell pepper mixture. Add the pine nuts and thyme. Drizzle with a little olive oil and season well.

6 Bake in a preheated oven, 400°F, for 18–20 minutes, or until the edges are crisp and golden. Cut into fingers and serve immediately.

Step *3*

Step *5*

Step *6*

French Bread Pizzas

Halved French sticks or Italian bread are a ready-made pizza base. The colors of the tomatoes and cheese contrast beautifully on top.

SERVES 4

INGREDIENTS

2 sticks of French bread
Tomato Sauce (page 192)
4 plum tomatoes, sliced thinly lengthwise
5 oz Mozzarella, sliced thinly
10 black olives, cut into rings
8 fresh basil leaves, shredded
olive oil for drizzling
salt and pepper

1 Cut the French bread in half lengthwise and toast the cut side of the bread lightly. Spread the toasted bread with the tomato sauce.

2 Arrange the tomato and Mozzarella slices alternately along the length.

3 Top with the olive rings and half the basil. Drizzle over a little olive oil and season well.

4 Either place under a preheated medium broiler and cook until the cheese is melted and bubbling or bake in a preheated oven, 400°F, for 15–20 minutes.

5 Sprinkle over the remaining basil and serve immediately.

Step *1*

Step *2*

Step *3*

Giardiniera

As the name implies, this colorful pizza should be topped with fresh vegetables from the garden, especially in the summer months.

SERVES 2-4

INGREDIENTS

6 spinach leaves
Potato Base (page 190)
Special Tomato Sauce (page 194)
1 tomato, sliced
1 celery stalk, sliced thinly
½ green bell pepper, sliced thinly
1 baby zucchini, sliced
1 oz asparagus tips
1 oz corn, defrosted if frozen
1 oz peas, defrosted if frozen
4 scallions, trimmed and chopped
1 tbsp chopped fresh mixed herbs
2 oz Mozzarella, grated
2 tbsp freshly grated Parmesan
1 artichoke heart
olive oil for drizzling
salt and pepper

1 Remove any tough stalks from the spinach and wash the leaves in plenty of cold water. Pat dry with paper towels.

2 Roll out or press the potato base, using a rolling pin or your hands, into a 10 in. round on a lightly floured counter. Place the round on a large greased cookie sheet or pizza pan and push up the edge a little. Spread with the tomato sauce.

3 Arrange the spinach leaves on the sauce, followed by the tomato slices. Top with the remaining vegetables and the herbs.

4 Mix together the cheeses and sprinkle over. Place the artichoke heart in the center. Drizzle the pizza with a little olive oil and season.

5 Bake in a preheated oven, 400°F, for 18–20 minutes, or until the edges are crisp and golden brown. Serve immediately.

Step *1*

Step *3*

Step *4*

Wild Mushroom & Walnut

Wild mushrooms make a delicious pizza topping when mixed with walnuts and Roquefort cheese.

SERVES 2-4

INGREDIENTS

Biscuit Base (page 188)
Special Tomato Sauce (page 194)
4 oz soft cheese
1 tbsp chopped fresh mixed herbs, such as parsley, oregano, and basil
8 oz wild mushrooms, such as oyster, shiitake, or ceps, or 4 oz each wild and button mushrooms
2 tbsp olive oil
¼ tsp fennel seeds
1 oz walnuts, chopped roughly
1½ oz blue cheese
olive oil for drizzling
salt and pepper
flat-leaf parsley sprig, to garnish

1 Roll out or press the biscuit base, using a rolling pin or your hands, into a 10 in. round on a lightly floured counter. Place on a large greased cookie sheet or pizza pan and push up the edge a little with your fingers to form a rim.

2 Spread with the tomato sauce almost to the edge. Dot with the soft cheese and herbs.

3 Wipe and slice the mushrooms. Heat the oil in a large skillet or wok and stir-fry the mushrooms and fennel seeds for 2–3 minutes. Spread over the pizza with the chopped walnuts.

4 Crumble the cheese over the pizza, drizzle with a little olive oil, and season.

5 Bake in a preheated oven, 400°F, for 18–20 minutes, or until the edge is crisp and golden. Serve immediately, garnished with a sprig of flat-leaf parsley.

Step *2*

Step *3*

Step *4*

Ratatouille & Lentil

The ideal vegetarian pizza. Ratatouille and lentils on a whole wheat bread base are topped with vegetarian cheese and sunflower seeds.

SERVES 2–4

INGREDIENTS

2 oz green lentils
½ small eggplant, diced
1 small onion, sliced
1 garlic clove, crushed
3 tbsp olive oil
½ zucchini, sliced
½ red bell pepper, sliced
½ green bell pepper, sliced
7 oz can chopped tomatoes
1 tbsp chopped fresh oregano or 1 tsp dried
Bread Dough Base made with
whole wheat flour (page 186)
2 oz vegetarian hard cheese, sliced thinly
1 tbsp sunflower seeds
olive oil for drizzling
salt and pepper

1 Soak the lentils in hot water for 30 minutes. Drain and rinse; then cover with fresh water, and simmer for 10 minutes.

2 Sprinkle the eggplant with a little salt in a colander and leave the bitter juices to drain for about 20 minutes. Rinse and pat dry with paper towels.

3 Fry the onion and garlic gently in the oil for 3 minutes. Add the zucchini, bell peppers, and eggplant. Cover and leave to cook over a low heat for about 5 minutes.

4 Add the tomatoes, drained lentils, oregano, 2 tablespoons of water, and seasoning. Cover and simmer for 15 minutes, stirring occasionally, adding more water if necessary.

5 Roll out or press the dough, using a rolling pin or your hands, into a 10 in. round on a lightly floured counter. Place on a large greased cookie sheet or pizza pan and push up the edge slightly. Cover and leave to rise slightly for 10 minutes in a warm place.

6 Spread the ratatouille over the dough base almost to the edge. Arrange the cheese slices on top and sprinkle over the sunflower seeds. Drizzle with a little olive oil and season.

7 Bake in a preheated oven, 400°F, for 18–20 minutes, or until the edge is crisp and golden brown. Serve immediately.

Step *1*

Step *3*

Step *6*

Tofu with Corn & Peas

*Chunks of tofu marinated in ginger and soy sauce impart something
of an oriental flavor to this pizza.*

SERVES 2-4

INGREDIENTS

4½ cups milk
1 tsp salt
8 oz semolina
1 tbsp soy sauce
1 tbsp dry sherry
½ tsp grated fresh ginger root
9 oz tofu, cut into chunks
2 eggs
2 oz Parmesan, grated
Tomato Sauce (page 192)
1 oz baby corncobs, cut into 4
1 oz snow peas, trimmed and cut into 4
4 scallions, trimmed and cut into
1 in. strips
2 oz Mozzarella, sliced thinly
2 tsp sesame oil
salt and pepper

1 Bring the milk to a boil with the salt. Sprinkle the semolina over the surface, stirring all the time. Cook for 10 minutes over a low heat, stirring occasionally, taking care not to let it burn. Remove from the heat and leave to cool until tepid.

2 Mix the soy sauce, sherry, and ginger together in a bowl, add the tofu, and stir gently to coat. Leave to marinate in a cool place for about 20 minutes.

3 Beat the eggs with a little pepper. Add to the semolina with the Parmesan and mix well. Place on a large greased cookie sheet or pizza pan and pat into a 10 in. round, using the back of a metal spoon. Spread the tomato sauce almost to the edge.

4 Blanch the corncobs and snow peas in boiling water for 1 minute, drain, and place on the pizza with the drained tofu. Top with the scallions and slices of cheese. Drizzle over the sesame oil and season.

5 Bake in a preheated oven, 400°F, for 18–20 minutes, or until the edge is crisp and golden. Serve immediately.

Step *1*

Step *2*

Step *4*

Three Cheese & Artichoke

Sliced artichokes combined with sharp hard cheese, Parmesan, and blue cheese give a really delicious topping to this pizza.

SERVES 2-4

INGREDIENTS

Bread Dough Base (page 186)
Special Tomato Sauce (page 194)
2 oz blue cheese, sliced
4 oz artichoke hearts in oil, sliced
½ small red onion, chopped
1½ oz sharp hard cheese, grated
2 tbsp freshly grated Parmesan
1 tbsp chopped fresh thyme
oil from artichokes for drizzling
salt and pepper

TO SERVE

salad greens
cherry tomatoes, halved

1 Roll out or press the dough, using a rolling pin or your hands, into a 10 in. round on a lightly floured counter. Place the base on a large greased cookie sheet or pizza pan and push up the edge slightly. Cover and leave to rise for 10 minutes in a warm place.

2 Spread with the tomato sauce almost to the edge. Arrange the blue cheese on the tomato sauce, followed by the artichoke hearts and red onion.

3 Mix the sharp hard cheese and Parmesan together with the thyme and sprinkle the mixture over the pizza. Drizzle a little of the oil from the jar of artichokes over the pizza and season to taste.

4 Bake in a preheated oven, 400°F, for 18–20 minutes, or until the edge is crisp and golden and the cheese is bubbling.

5 Serve immediately with fresh salad greens and cherry tomato halves.

Step 2

Step 3

Step 5

DESSERTS

Many Italians prefer to finish their meal with a bowl of mixed fruits or fruits with cheese, but they do like their desserts, too. When there is a family gathering or celebration, then a special effort is made and the delicacies appear. The Sicilians are said to have the sweetest tooth of all, and many Italian desserts are thought to have originated there. You have to go a very long way to beat a Sicilian ice-cream, especially the famous cassata and Ricotta ice-creams.

Fruits also feature in desserts. The mouthwatering pear tarts from northern Italy use the very best fruit blended with apricot jelly, raisins, and almonds. Oranges are often peeled and served whole, marinated in a fragrant syrup and liqueur. Almond-flavored cookies are often served as an accompaniment, and the famous Florentines – cookies packed with candied fruit and covered with chocolate – are a special favorite. Gâteaux are popular, often incorporating Mascarpone, Italian full-fat cream cheese, or Ricotta cheese, together with citrus fruits, and honey. Tiramisu is an all-time favorite, and for Christmas and special occasions try the honey cake from Siena called Panforte – so very rich that even a tiny piece will leave you with delicious memories for a very long time.

Tiramisu

A favorite Italian dessert flavored with coffee and Amaretto. You could
replace the Amaretto with brandy or Marsala.

SERVES 4–6

INGREDIENTS

20–24 lady-fingers, about 5 oz
2 tbsp cold black coffee
2 tbsp coffee essence
2 tbsp Amaretto
4 egg yolks
6 tbsp superfine sugar
few drops of vanilla extract
grated rind of ½ lemon
1½ cups Italian full-fat cream cheese
2 tsp lemon juice
1 cup heavy cream
1 tbsp milk
½ cup slivered almonds, lightly toasted
2 tbsp cocoa powder
1 tbsp confectioners' sugar

1 Arrange almost half the lady-fingers in the base of a glass bowl or serving dish.

2 Combine the black coffee, coffee essence, and Amaretto and sprinkle just a little more than half of the mixture over the fingers.

3 Put the egg yolks into a heatproof bowl with the sugar, vanilla extract, and lemon rind. Stand over a saucepan of gently simmering water and beat until very thick and creamy and the whisk leaves a very heavy trail when lifted from the bowl.

4 Put the cream cheese in a bowl with the lemon juice and beat until smooth.

5 Combine the egg and cream cheese mixtures, and when evenly blended, pour half over the lady-fingers, and spread out evenly.

6 Add another layer of fingers, sprinkle with the remaining coffee, and then cover with the rest of the cheese mixture. Chill for at least 2 hours and preferably longer, or overnight.

7 To serve, whip the cream and milk together until fairly stiff and spread or pipe over the dessert. Sprinkle with the slivered almonds and then sift an even layer of cocoa powder so the top is completely covered. Finally sift a light layer of confectioners' sugar over the cocoa.

Step *2*

Step *3*

Step *6*

Zabaglione

Serve this light dessert warm or chilled, accompanied by lady-fingers or amaretti cookies, and soft fruits.

SERVES 4

INGREDIENTS

6 egg yolks
6 tbsp superfine sugar
6 tbsp Marsala
amaretti cookies or lady-fingers (optional)
strawberries or raspberries (optional)

1 Put the egg yolks into a heatproof bowl and whip until a pale yellow color, using a rotary, balloon, or electric whisk.

2 Beat in the sugar, followed by the Marsala, continuing to whip all the time.

3 Stand the bowl over a saucepan of very gently simmering water, or transfer to the top of a double boiler, and continue to beat until the mixture thickens sufficiently to stand in soft peaks. On no account allow the water to boil or the zabaglione will overcook and turn into scrambled eggs.

4 Scrape around the sides of the bowl from time to time while beating. As soon as the mixture is really thick and foamy, take from the heat and continue to beat for a couple of minutes longer.

5 Pour immediately into stemmed glasses and serve warm; or leave until cold and serve chilled.

6 Fruits, such as strawberries or raspberries, or crumbled lady-fingers or amaretti cookies may be placed in the base of the glasses before adding the zabaglione.

Step *1*

Step *2*

Step *4*

Ricotta Ice-Cream

Ice-cream is a traditional Italian dish, and the numerous flavors are available usually sold in a cone. However, it is also served sliced.

SERVES 4–6

INGREDIENTS

¼ cup pistachio nuts
¼ cup walnuts or pecan nuts
¼ cup toasted chopped hazelnuts
grated rind of 1 orange
grated rind of 1 lemon
2 tbsp candied or stem ginger
2 tbsp candied cherries
¼ cup dried apricots
3 tbsp raisins
1½ cups Ricotta
2 tbsp Maraschino, Amaretto, or brandy
1 tsp vanilla extract
4 egg yolks
½ cup superfine sugar

TO DECORATE

whipped cream
a few candied cherries, pistachio nuts,
or mint leaves

1 Roughly chop the pistachio nuts and walnuts and mix with the toasted hazelnuts, orange and lemon rind. Finely chop the ginger, cherries, apricots, and raisins, and add to the bowl.

2 Stir the Ricotta evenly through the fruit mixture, then beat in the liqueur and vanilla extract.

3 Put the egg yolks and sugar in a bowl and beat hard until very thick and creamy – they may be beaten over a pan of gently simmering water to speed up the process. Leave to cool if necessary.

4 Carefully fold the Ricotta mixture evenly through the beaten eggs and sugar until smooth.

5 Line a 17 × 5 in. loaf pan with a double layer of plastic wrap or baking parchment. Pour in the Ricotta mixture, level the top, cover with more plastic wrap or baking parchment, and chill in the freezer until firm, at least overnight.

6 To serve, carefully remove the ice-cream from the pan and peel off the paper. Place on a serving dish and decorate with whipped cream, candied cherries, pistachio nuts, and/or mint leaves. Serve in slices.

Step *1*

Step *4*

Step *5*

Caramelized Oranges

The secret of these oranges is to allow them to marinate in the syrup for at least 24 hours, so the flavors amalgamate.

SERVES 6

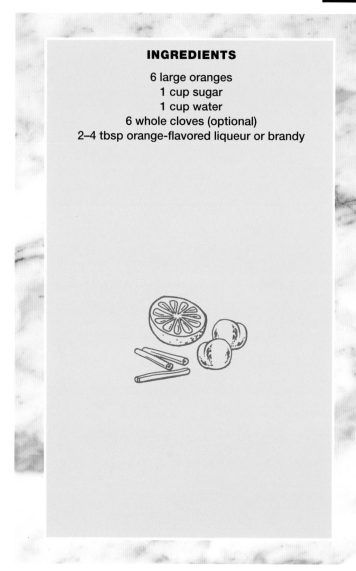

INGREDIENTS

6 large oranges
1 cup sugar
1 cup water
6 whole cloves (optional)
2–4 tbsp orange-flavored liqueur or brandy

1 Using a citrus zester or potato peeler, pare the rind from 2 of the oranges in narrow strips without any white pith attached. If using a potato peeler, cut the peel into very thin julienne strips.

2 Put the strips into a small saucepan and barely cover with water. Bring to a boil and simmer for 5 minutes. Drain the strips and reserve the water.

3 Cut away all the white pith and peel from the remaining oranges using a very sharp knife. Then cut horizontally into 4 slices. Reassemble the oranges and hold in place with wooden toothpicks. Stand in a heatproof dish.

4 Put the sugar and water into a heavy-based saucepan with the cloves, if using. Bring to a boil and simmer gently until the sugar has dissolved, then boil hard without stirring until the syrup thickens and begins to color. Continue to cook until a light golden brown, then quickly remove from the heat, and carefully pour in the reserved orange rind liquid.

5 Place over a gentle heat until the caramel has fully dissolved again, then remove from the heat, and add the liqueur or brandy. Pour over the oranges.

6 Sprinkle the orange strips over the oranges, cover with plastic wrap, and leave until cold. Chill for at least 3 hours and preferably for 24–48 hours before serving. If time allows, spoon the syrup over the oranges several times while they are marinating. Discard the toothpicks before serving.

Step *3*

Step *5*

Step *6*

Pear Tart

*Pears are a very popular fruit in Italy. In this recipe from Trentino they
are flavored with almonds, cinnamon, raisins, and apricot jelly*

SERVES 4–6

INGREDIENTS

2¼ cups all-purpose flour
pinch of salt
½ cup superfine sugar
½ cup butter, diced
1 egg
1 egg yolk
few drops of vanilla extract
2–3 tsp water
sifted confectioners' sugar, for sprinkling

FILLING

4 tbsp apricot jelly
2 oz amaretti or ratafia cookies, crumbled
1¾–2 lb pears, peeled and cored
1 tsp ground cinnamon
½ cup raisins
⅓ cup soft brown or
demerara sugar

1 Sift the flour and salt onto a flat surface, make a well in the center, and add the sugar, butter, egg, egg yolk, vanilla extract, and most of the water.

2 Using your fingers gradually work the flour into the other ingredients to give a smooth, pliable dough, adding a little more water if necessary. Wrap in plastic wrap and chill for 1 hour or until firm. Alternatively, put all the ingredients into a food processor and process until evenly blended and smooth.

3 Roll out about three-quarters of the dough and use to line a shallow 10 in. cake pan or deep flan pan. Spread the apricot jelly over the base and sprinkle with the crushed cookies.

4 Slice the pears very thinly. Arrange over the cookies in the pastry case. Sprinkle first with cinnamon, then with raisins, and finally with the brown sugar.

5 Roll out a thin sausage shape using about one-third of the remaining dough, and place around the edge of the pie. Roll the remainder into thin sausages and arrange in a lattice over the pie, 4 or 5 strips in each direction, attaching them to the strip around the edge.

6 Cook in a preheated oven, 400°F, for about 50 minutes until golden brown and cooked through. Remove from the oven and leave to cool. Serve warm or chilled, sprinkled with sifted confectioners' sugar.

Step *1*

Step *3*

Step *5*

Panforte di Siena

This famous Tuscan honey and nut cake is a Christmas speciality. In Italy it is sold in pretty boxes, and served in very thin slices.

SERVES 12

INGREDIENTS

1 cup split whole almonds
¾ cup hazelnuts
½ cup cut mixed peel
⅓ cup no-need-to-soak dried apricots
2 oz candied pineapple
grated rind of 1 large orange
½ cup all-purpose flour
2 tbsp cocoa powder
2 tsp ground cinnamon
½ cup superfine sugar
½ cup honey
confectioners' sugar, for dredging

1 Toast the almonds under the broiler until lightly browned and place in a bowl. Toast the hazelnuts until the skins split. Place on a dry dishcloth and rub off the skins. Roughly chop the hazelnuts and add to the almonds with the mixed peel.

2 Chop the apricots and pineapple fairly finely, add to the nuts with the orange rind, and mix well.

3 Sift the flour with the cocoa and cinnamon, add to the nut mixture, and mix evenly.

4 Line a round 8 in. cake pan or deep loose-based flan pan with baking parchment.

5 Put the sugar and honey into a saucepan and heat until the sugar dissolves, then boil gently for about 5 minutes or until the mixture thickens and begins to turn a deeper shade of brown. Quickly add to the nut mixture and mix evenly. Turn into the prepared pan and level the top using the back of a damp spoon.

6 Cook in a preheated oven, 300°F, for 1 hour. Remove from the oven and leave in the pan until cold. Take out of the pan and carefully peel off the paper. Before serving, dredge the cake heavily with sifted confectioners' sugar. Serve in very thin slices.

Step *1*

Step *2*

Step *5*

INDEX